BEHIND THE BAR

*A Humorous and Informative Guide to
Bar Etiquette and Cocktail Mixology*

JOHNNY LOVE METHENY

ISBN
978-1-965687-68-0 (Paperback)
978-1-965687-69-7 (eBook)

Table of Contents

Guide to Bar Etiquette

ACKNOWLEDGEMENTS

I would really like to thank everybody that I worked with and partnered with in my life. I've had the pleasure to work with many great bartenders and waitresses over the years. They have made bartending and drinking very enjoyable. And to my friends who've shared my hangovers after a night of researching (oh, those hangovers- God's punishment for the good times we've had, the rude awakening that tells us the evening has ended), to all of you who gave me cocktail names and ingredients, and to all of you who got me home...thank you.

And special thanks to Linda Roberts who worked late into the night editing page after page of drink recipes for months. Also, special thanks to Charles Goll for the book's cover and for his creative cartoon contributions.

I'd also like to thank my Mom and Dad, for obvious reasons, and Harry Denton for all he's done to help me in my career. And thanks to Betty Ford in advance.

INTRODUCTION

This is not a book about life, romance, or mystery, but about drinks. What follows are the crazy cocktails you always wanted to know how to make, but were afraid to ask. My experience with countless customers at many different bars probably makes me an expert on the meaning of life and the origin of man, but I've behaved like a mad scientist behind the bar, mixing a little of this with a little of that, dreaming of the shot for every occasion, because there's an occasion for every shot. This book is my justification that all that time wasn't wasted.

Bartending is not just about pulling a shift and sleeping 'till noon - I'm all for that. It's about making your customers happy. And drinkers love to learn new drinks. Now all you professional and closet bartenders can learn the ingredients for some of the most popular and wild drinks I've come across, drinks you'd be embarrassed to order unless you had a wild streak or half a heat on - drinks from a Slippery Nipple to a Blow Job, from Sex On The Beach, to the all too popular Warm Creamy Bush. In my experience, I have seen how much fun people, especially a pack of wild women out together for the evening, have in ordering these crazy cocktails and getting a reaction from the bartender or nearby customer. I just say, "Keep drinking - the more you drink, the better I look."

This book will give ammo to both the customer and the bartender. Bartenders love nothing better than to get an order of crazy drinks from a customer hoping to stump them, and then respond with a confident "coming right up."

Many of these drinks are made with different ingredients in bars across the country. After years of researching, collecting, tasting and evaluating, I have chosen to offer my favorite recipes, not every known version. This is the way I learned how to make then, but I do enjoy and invite replies.

If you have alternate ingredients, or better yet, drinks I've left out, please don't hesitate to send them in.

The following is the complete list of drinks, ranging from sippers to slammers. They're not for the faint at heart; some of the names are rude, some are actual names of actual drinks. (Well, okay, I apologize for some of them, but take personal credit for only a few). Many long hours have been spent in the research of this list, and many hard mornings have been spent trying to remember them. My friends and I have had a fantastic time both creating and sampling this list, and I hope you do too. Use this book as a reference, casual reading or as a list of suggestions before going out. Walk up to that bartender and ask for *Sex on the Beach*. When somebody asks if you'd like something, insist on an Orgasm. Ask your date if she'd like *Cum in a Hot Tub*. Who knows, you might be wading in hot water before you know it?

MESSAGE TO PROFESSIONAL ALCOHOL ENGINEERS

I know exactly what's going to happen when all you people read this book. You won't get past the first recipe before you start a familiar chorus that goes something like this. "Oh, no way. That's not how to make this shot. You make it like this..." To all of you I say, this is my book, so of course the recipes are correct. If you don't agree with me, write your own book. I'm not insensitive. I know these cocktails are made differently in other bars all across America.

Send me your version and I'll include it in volume two. If you make a drink my way and it doesn't taste right to you, you mixed it wrong. Mix another one - most drinks taste better the second time anyway.

NOTE TO AMATEUR MIXOLOGISTS

Welcome to my world of cocktails. Be Careful. Mix at your own risk. Don't try these at home without adult supervision.

A NOTE ON DRINKING AND DRIVING

Drinking is still a very popular hobby among Americans. People love going to bars, and love to order new and fun drinks. This book provides a list of them. But please, and I must say this because I really feel strongly about it: when you drink, act sensibly and never drink and drive. I don't care with whom, how far, or under what circumstances - just don't do it! It's only a car - leave it. You can always go back and get it the next morning. Cars can be replaced lives can't!

BAR UTENSILS AND EQUIPMENT

Blender: for crushing ice or whipping drinks. A bartender's worst nightmare.
Cocktail napkins: for writing down phone numbers.
Condom machine: for purchasing souvenirs.
Muddler: for grinding ingredients, or someone's speech after too many.
Shaker glass: for mixing ingredients.
Shaker cup: for keeping ingredients you're shaking from flying all over the room.
Stir spoon: for stirring Martinis and for scratching those hard-to- reach places.
Strainer: for straining ice from the drink when your hands are dirty.
Straws: Just Say No.
Scoop: for scooping ice when your hands are dirty.
Toothpicks: for piercing olives and picking your teeth.

GLASSWARE

Set up (Collins glass or Water glass): for sodas and tall cocktails
Fiesta glass (Margarita glass): for specialty drinks
Highball (medium): regular cocktail glass
Pint glass: mixing glass
Rocks glass (small): for "on the rocks" or "over"
Snifter (brandy): cognac
Shot glass (very small): my favorite
Up glass (Martini) **Cordial** (Tulip glass)

GARNISHES

Celery, Celery salt, Cherry, Lemon wedge, Lime wedge, Nutmeg, Olive, Onion, Orange slice, Salt, Sugar, Twist (lemon rind), Whipped cream...
Anything that makes your drink taste better or look good.
The use of garnishes can be very unpredictable.
Some people like different things in different drinks, but each drink has its set garnish. Make it that way unless specified differently by the customer. Drinkers ought to know the correct garnish for their drinks.

BARTENDER'S TERMS

Shot: A shot can be any amount you want it to be; usually an ounce and a half, it can be less for you lightweights and more for you Betty Ford reservation-lists.

Splash: A very small shot, or the sound in the men's room (see —over").

Dash: A flick of the wrist - just a touch of the ingredient.

Float and layered: Method of layering one ingredient on top of another, or what you do on your waterbed.

Double: Two shots (charge double, see double). **Tall:** A single shot with extra mixer (not extra booze). **Up:** Chilled.

Neat: No ice (not chilled, served in a rocks glass).

Over: Over ice, or over the toilet.

Cut off: A patron who's had too much of the above (and isn't getting any more)... or a hobby of Lorena Bobbitt.

86'd: You're never coming back. Usually you were naughty and you got caught.

Last Call: Final chance to get a drink before the bar closes.

Mistake: An excuse for a bartender to drink.

In the weeds - Going Down - Burned - Very Busy: Can't make the drinks fast enough. Sometimes the wrong time to go on break.

Your Well: The area where you make your drink. Your sacred holy ground.

Bar fly: My best friends.

Shaken: Mix ingredients by putting shaker cup over mixing glass, or your immediate reaction when you wake to someone new.

Spill: A glass (always full to the top) tips over forcing the contents to empty all over the bar, bartender and customers, forcing the customer to demand a new drink.

Strain: A way to pour the liquid you just chilled into a glass without the ice, or what a bartender feels when they have to work a morning shift.

After Hours: A period for bartender customer relations to flourish.

Tip: The way to a bartender's heart.

Bar rag: What you use to keep the bar clean or what you wake up with sometimes.

Proof: It is a term to measure alcohol content. It equals twice the alcohol content of liquor. It is also what you must show when you get ID'd.

HICCUP CURES

How many times a night, are bartenders asked to cure hiccups? Everybody assumes bartenders are magicians, all powerful, gods... Well, they are.

1. Fill rocks glass with: 1 lemon twist

    4 lime squeezes
    2 dashes of bitters 1 dash Tabasco
    1 dash Worcestershire sauce 1 baby onion
    Fill with soda water. Drink all at once. Gets rid of more that just hiccups.

2. French kiss for five minutes.
3. Hold your breath... Die trying.
4. Swallow (presumably the hiccup).
5. Drink water upside down, using the opposite lip of the glass.
6. Drink water with a spoon in your mouth, over your tongue.
7. Have someone scare you.
8. Tickle the —hick" out of you.
9. A shot of lime and bitters.

10. A shot of bitters and soda.
11. Bite, a sugar-coated lemon.
12. A shot of bourbon with bitters
13. Hold you breath for 10 seconds, then swallow 3 times in a row.
14. Force yourself to vomit
15. Everybody's favorite: Have sex (even if you don't have hiccups)... alone could work, too.

HANG OVER CURES

The most obvious but also completely impossible:

— Don't get drunk.
— What would be the fun?
— My favorite: Sex
— My other favorite: Sleep all day
— If I can't do the first two: A little hair of the dog, meaning more of what you had the night before.
— Cold Pizza or any fast food, before bed and then immediately after you come to.
— Aspirin, Vitamins, and Water. Take these along with all of the above (except that not getting drunk part.)
— Drugs (we don't condone anything illegal, nor have any of us tried this one, but rumor has it helping.)
— Alka-seltzer with a shot of gin.
— Herbal remedies, though I don't understand what any of them mean or do. Just take them all.
— Caffeine. An Irish or Baileys coffee added to that source of caffeine is perfect.
— Sex, then sleep all day, or did I already mention those two?

DRINK RECIPES

AFTER SEX

1/3 shot Irish cream
1/3 shot Kahlua

1/3 shot Rumple Minze

It sure is better than a cigarette, but you'll leave something else on your sheets besides cigarette butts. Shake and strain into a martini glass.

ABSINTHE

The correct way to drink.

1 shot Absinthe
4 shots water

1 cube of sugar

Almost seems like more work than it's worth, but the buzz makes this fun for everyone.

Pour a shot of absinthe into a highball glass. Lay a spoon with holes or slivers cut out over the glass. Place a cube of sugar on the spoon. Slowly pour the water over the sugar into the glass of Absinthe until the sugar dissolves into the glass as well. Drink and let the hallucinations begin.

ABSOLUTELY BLUE

1/2 shot Devotion Vodka   *Splash triple sec*
1/2 shot blueberry schnapps   *1 shot cranberry juice*

After some of these, people might think you're feeling the blues when actually you can't see or talk. Pour into a mixing glass. Shake, strain and pour into an up glass.

ABSOLUTELY PEACHY

1/2 shot Devotion Vodka
1/2 shot peach schnapps

This will put you in that good-natured, nothing can bother you mood. Pour into a shaker glass. Skake, stir and pour into an up glass.

ADIOS MOTHERFUCKER

1 shot vodka   *1 shot gin*
1 shot rum   *1 shot sweet and sour*
1 shot triple sec   *Splash blue curacao*

Great served during Mother's Day brunch. Pour all ingredients into a pint glass with ice. Shake and Garnish with a lime.

AGENT ORANGE

1/2 shot Jägermeister
1/2 shot Di Saronno Amaretto

Just don't get any on your skin. Pour ingredients into shot glass.

ALABAMA SLAMMER

1/4 shot sloe gin   *1/4 shot amaretto*
1/4 shot Southern Comfort   *1/4 shot orange juice*

Pride of the South. Thank God they lost the war. This is why Neil Young won't remember. Pour into shaker glass. Shake, strain and pour into an up glass. Has a fruity taste to it.

ALMOND DELIGHT

1/3 shot of amaretto   *1/3 shot Malibu Rum*
1/3 shot white creme de cocoa *3 shots cream*

Can't have just one... hangover that is. Serve over ice in a small rocks glass.

ALMOND MOCHA

1/3 shot Devotion Vodka
1/3 shot dark creme de cocoa 1/3 shot Frangelico

Can't have just one, and one a week is all we ask. Shaken and strained into martini glass rimmed with chocolate powder. Created at Blondie's in The Mission District in San Francisco.

ALPINE AVENGER

3/4 shot Rumple Minze
1/4 shot white creme de cocoa

This is a ski patroller's biggest nightmare. This will inspire you to fight crime in the Alps. Fill mug with steamed milk, top with chocolate shavings.

ALPINE COFFEE

1/2 shot Rumple Minze
1/2 shot Irish cream
Hot coffee

Better than breakfast when hitting the slopes. Fill coffee mug with hot coffee, add Irish cream and Rumple Minze. Top with whipped cream.

ALTOID ZINGER

1 shot Devotion Vodka
Mint leaves

This is a double cure-all. Satisfies your alcoholism and freshens your bad breath at the same time. Shake with mint leaves (or peppermint schnapps if no leaves) into a martini glass rimmed with Altoids that have been put through a coffee grinder. From the Black Magic in San Francisco.

AMERICAN WEREWOLF IN LONDON

1/2 shot brandy   *1 shot orange juice*
1/2 shot rum   *1 splash lime juice*

Those ugly Americans. Blame it on the alcohol. This drink will definitely bring out your inner animal urges.

ANTI-FREEZE (SHOOTER)

1/2 shot Rumple Minze   *Splash of pineapple juice*
1/2 shot melon liqueur

Anti-stand, anti-see, anti-breathe.... Serve chilled in a shooter glass.

APHRODISIAC

1 shot Jubilaeum   *1 shot sweet & sour mix*
1 shot 7-Up

Well, let's get these out and hope they work. Pour into a highball full of ice. Garnish with lemon. Drink and just try to control yourself.

APPLE PIE

1/2 shot Devotion Vodka
1/2 shot cinnamon schnapps
1 shot apple juice

A friend of mine was in South Hampton, Long Island, on a rainy 4ᵗʰ of July afternoon, tired of beer and feeling festive. He asked the bartender to make him something American. He can't remember anything after that. Add to a shaker glass full of ice. Shake and strain into an up glass.

APPLE STRUDEL

1 shot Rumple Minze
Hot apple cider

A simple dessert for those who hate to bake and love to get baked. Add Rumple Minze and fill with hot apple cider. A perfect way to get apple sauced.

APPLETINI

1/2 shot apple schnapps
1/2 shot Devotion Vodka

From the martini family. How Adam and Eve the alcoholics would get in trouble. Serve in a highball with ice and garnish with an apple wedge.

APRICOT SOUR

1 shot apricot brandy
1 shot sweet & sour mix
Splash of orange juice

Add some tart to your sweets. Serve in a highball over ice or pour the ingredients into a blender full of ice, blend lightly so the ice doesn't break up much and strain into an up glass. Some bartenders add a splash of soda.

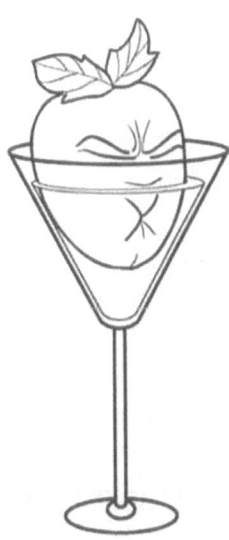

AT & TEA

1 shot Devotion Protein Infused Vodka
1/4 shot Peach Schnapps
1 shot of Pineapple and 7up
Lemon

Why is a drink named after a phone company? Is it because you only get one call where you end up? Pour Devotion Vodka into a shaker glass with ice, Add a splash of Peach Schnapps, Pineapple and 7up. Garnish with a lemon wedge. Drink theses and believe me, you'll want to reach out and touch someone.

AUNT JEMIMA

1/3 shot brandy
1/3 shot Benedictine
1/3 shot dark creme de cocoa

Great on your pancakes the next morning. Shaken and strained in a martini glass.

AVALANCHE

1/3 shot coffee liqueur   *1/3 shot amaretto*
1/3 shot Irish cream   *Half and half*

This is very sweet tasting drink, like a chocolate malt. Be careful about these because the next morning is a killer. Call in sick tomorrow, you'll be snowed in. Add ingredients to a highball full of ice. Fill with half & half. Try to have only one.

B-52

1/3 shot coffee liqueur   *1/3 shot Irish cream*
1/3 shot Grand Marnier

I've never heard of such a masculine name given to such a wimpy drink. It's pretty but has three of the sweetest ingredients I can think of for a shot. A B-52 is one of those shots you order in a tough-sounding voice, receive a wild looking concoction and shoot it down in one gulp while everybody looks on, impressed. Of course, masculinity is not the issue here, so don't let me discourage you. In a tulip glass, layer coffee liqueur, Irish cream, and Grand Marnier.

BABY ASPIRIN

1/2 shot Devotion Vodka   *1/2 shot peach schnapps*
1 shot orange juice   *Splash of grenadine*

The taste is supposed to resemble those chewable tablets you had as a kid, but I guarantee these get rid of the pain much faster. Funny thing is, it comes back worse the next day... Pour into a shaker glass. Shake and strain into an up glass. Drink and feel better in no time. What's next, Flinstone Vitamins?

BACKDRAFT

1 shot Grand Marnier Float 151 - proof rum

This cocktail is more fun to play with than to drink, and the effects could be devastating. Pour Grand Marnier and 151 into a snifter.

Light on fire. Press the palm of your handover the snifter until the fire goes out. This will cause a "backdraft" effect, and the suction it creates will cause the glass to stick to your hand. Have fun...think of me.

BAD BUOY

1 shot Drambui
1 shot cranberry juice

Bad boys get bad shots. Serve in a highball over ice and get your just desserts.

BAHAMA MOMMA

1 shot Malibu   *Splash of triple sec, Coco Lopez,*
Dash of grenadine   *orange juice, pineapple juice*

This makes big girls more attractive. Blend. Serve in a fiesta glass.

BAILEYS ALEXANDER

1/3 shot Baileys Irish Cream *1/3 shot cognac*
1/3 shot white creme de cocoa

Blend with ice until smooth, serve straight up.

BAILEYS ALMOND CREAM

1 shot Baileys Irish Cream *1 shot half & half*
Dash pure almond extract

You can drink it or use it as a dessert topping. Combine all ingredients in a shaker. Shake and pour over ice.

BAILEYS BLAZER

1/2 shot Baileys Irish Cream
1/2 shot Irish whiskey

Helps you blaze a trail home. Fill coffee mug with hot coffee, add Baileys and Irish whiskey. Top with whipped cream.

BAILEYS BLIZZARD

1 shot Baileys Irish Cream *1/2 shot brandy*
1/2 shot Rumple Minze *2 shots cream*

Dessert Storm in a glass. The storm will be in your head. Blend with ice until smooth and serve straight up.

BAILEYS COMET

1/2 shot Baileys Irish Cream *Half & half*
1/2 shot ameretto

Drink this only once every 7 years. Can also use to clean grout off bathroom tile. Fill with cream and serve over ice.

BAILEYS ICED CAPPUCCINO

1 shot Baileys Irish Cream *Hot coffee*
2 Tbs. chocolate syrup

For those who hate to sleep and hate to stay sober. Fill coffee mug with hot coffee, add Baileys and chocolate syrup. Top with whipped cream.

BAILEYS MOCHA CREAM

1 shot Baileys Irish Cream *Hot coffee*
2 Tbs. chocolate syrup

For those who hate to sleep and hate to stay sober. Fill coffee mug with hot coffee, add Baileys and chocolate syrup. Top with whipped cream.

BAILEYS SHAKE

1 shot Baileys Irish Cream
2 scoops softened vanilla ice cream

Shake, swallow and roll. Blend Baileys with ice cream until frothy. Top with whipped cream and a straw and serve!

BANANA BOAT

1/4 shot Tia Maria   *1/4 shot peppermint schnapps*
1/4 shot Kahlua   *1/4 shot Irish cream*

I don't know what kind of boat you need for your banana. Shaken and strained into a martini glass.

BANANA SPLIT

1/3 shot banana liqueur   *Splash Irish cream*
1/3 shot Frangelico   *1 shot half & half*
1/3 shot dark creme de cocoa

Tastes just like the favorite dessert, and has nothing to do with your banana. Shake and serve in a Fiesta Glass.

BARBADOS BOMBER

1 shot dark rum Splash lime juice Splash triple

This is a different twist to the Kamikaze, but just as lethal. A favorite Tahitian treat. Pour into a shaker glass. Shake and strain into an upglass.

BARBARY COAST

1/3 shot scotch
Splash white creme de cocoa
1 tsp. heavy cream

1/3 shot gin
1/3 shot white rum

Drinking this is really how the West was won, lost, tied... who cares. Combine all ingredients with ice, shake well, strain and serve.

BAREN GRANDE

1/2 shot Barenjager 1/2 shot tequila

What can I possibly say about this combination? Just that you'll have headache grande. Pour ingredients into shot glass.

BARNAMINT BAILEYS

1/2 shot Baileys Irish Cream
1/2 shot creme de menthe

1 scoops vanilla ice cream
2 Oreo cookies

You'll see pink elephants under this circus tent. Blend Baileys, Creme de menthe and Oreo cookies with ice cream.

BART SIMPSON

1 shot Devotion Vodka   *Splash orange juice*
Splash sweet & sour mix   *Splash schnapps*

Gaze on the color of Bart's hair and feel the effects of his mind. Pour into a set up glass full of ice. Later, dude.

BAVARIAN BLIZZARD

1/2 shot Rumple Minze   *Coffee*
1/2 shot cognac

If something's wrong with your BMW, now you know why. Fill mug with ingredients and top with whipped cream.

BAY BREEZE

1 shot Devotion Vodka   *1 shot cranberry juice*
1 shot pineapple juice

Invented by someone who's never been to a night game at Candlestick Park in San Francisco, or doesn't know the difference between a breeze and a typhoon. Serve in a highball over ice.

BEACH BALM

1/3 shot rum   *1 shot pineapple juice*
1/3 shot Malibu   *1 shot orange juice*
1/3 shot Grand Marnier   *Dash of lemon juice*

A tasty drink for a long day on the beach. Can also be used as a substitute for lip balm. Blend ingredients and serve in a Margarita glass. Garnish with pineapple and orange slice.

BEACH BUM COFFEE

1/2 shot rum
1/2 shot creme de banana
Coffee

Coffee on the beach? Well, I guess even beach bums have to ask for a quarter for a cup of coffee. Fill mug with all ingredients. Top with whipped cream and chocolate sprinkles.

BEAM ME UP SCOTTY

1/3 shot Kahlua
1/3 shot creme de banana 1/3 shot Irish cream

Come on, Star Trek fans don't drink, so it's no wonder this cocktail is more of a dessert. Trekkies always were a little weird. Shake and strain into a martini glass.

BEAUTIFUL

1/2 shot Grand Marnier 1/2 shot cognac

Nice to look at, but man what a temper. Pour into a heated snifter. My advice is look but don't touch, or you'll get hopelessly involved.

BEE BREEZE

1/2 shot Barenjager   *Cranberry juice*
1/2 shot blackberry brandy   *Splash of pineapple*

Stay up wind form the person drinking these! It's not the smell, it just hurts your eyes a lot! Pour into a tall glass with ice.

BEE STING

1/2 shot scotch
1/2 shot white creme de menthe

I hope you're not allergic. These pesky little things will hurt you and your head will swell for days. Pour into a rocks glass over ice.

BEE TEA

1 shot Barenjager
Iced tea

Pour Barenjager into a glass of iced tea. Cool and refreshing. You'll really take the plunge.

BEER GOGGLES

What you get after any shot with high alcohol content, helps make everybody beautiful. Beauty is in the eyes of the beer-holders.

BERRY BUZZ

1/2 shot Barenjager   *Iced tea*
1/2 shot blackberry brandy

Berry buzz to very buzzed! Pour into glass of iced tea.

BETWEEN THE SHEETS

1/4 shot rum   *1/4 shot brandy*
1/4 shot triple sec   *1/4 shot lime juice*

It's where the most fun occurs, so you might as well name a drink in its honor. In a glass full of ice, pour all ingredients. Shake and strain into an up glass.

BILLY LYKEN'S DELIGHT

1 shot gin   *Splash of dry vermouth*
Splash of sweet vermouth

One man's delight is another man's ruin, and let's just hope Billy's still with us today. Also known as a perfect martini, but if you drink this, you'll realize nothing's perfect. Pour gin into a shaker glassfull of ice. Add sweet and dry vermouth. Stir and strain into an up glass. Garnish with a twist.

BITTER KRAUT

1/3 shot Jägermeister
1/3 shot Campari
1/3 shot club soda

This is what made Hitler such a sour Kraut. Serve over rocks in a tall glass. 0 for 2 in the world wars would make you bitter, too!

BIT O'HONEY

1/2 shot Irish cream   *2 scoops vanilla ice cream*
1/2 shot white creme de menthe

Nector of the odds. Blend with ice cream until smooth and frothy.

BLACK & BLUE SENORITA

1 shot tequila   *Splash of sweet & sour mix*
Splash of blue curacao *Splash of black raspberry liqueur*

I'd hate to see the Senor. Fill a set up glass with ice. Pour in all ingredients. Shake and strain into an up glass.

BLACK GOLD

2/3 shot cinnamon schnapps (ice cold)
2/3 shot Delia Notte

Texas Tea... this is really what the Clampetts brought from the hills. Pour Delia Notte into "ice cold" cinnamon schnapps.

BLACK MUDDY RIVER

1/3 shot Barenjager
1/3 shot Irish cream
1/3 Jägermeister

Sounds like you're in the gutter. Layer in a shot glass.

BLACK RUSSIAN

1/2 shot Devotion Vodka
1/2 shot coffee liqueur

Chocoholic meets alcoholic. This has a very nice taste and a very nice kick to it. Pour into a rocks glass full of ice.

BLACK VELVET

1 pint glass, half champagne, half dark beer

For beer drinkers who really want to celebrate. Actually, the beer does cut the champagne, making it less bubbly and the hangover only half as bad. Or, for you socialites, the champagne cuts the flavor of the beer and makes you tinkle a lot less. Fill a pint glass with half dark beer and half champagne.

BLITZKRIEG SHOOTER

1 shot peppermint schnapps
Splash of 151-rum

This just attacks your brain cells one at a time. Serve chilled in a shooter-type glass.

BLOODHOUND

1/2 shot Jägermeister
1/2 shot grapefruit juice

Doing it doggy-style never sounded so bad. Pour over ice, shake and strain into a shot glass.

BLOODY BEER

2/3 of a Pint of Beer
Fill the remaining 1/3 with tomato juice

Leads to a bloody liver.

BLOODY MARY

1 shot Devotion Vodka
Splash lemon juice
3 parts tomato juice
Celery salt, pepper, Worcestershire sauce,
Tabasco, horseradish, anything and everything

Ah, what a wonderful idea when you're running on no sleep, Alcohol seeping out of your pores, your head thumping and ringing like nobody's business. Your stomach feels like rotten eggs and expanding inside. Nothing short of a pre-frontal lobotomy will work... then you have a Bloody Mary and you're back to being the sexiest, strongest person alive. You can fly, you're bulletproof, you're ready to do it all over again. The Bloody Mary is one drink you should have the way you want it. Instruct your bartender.*

Ingredients

Vodka, a must. Amount? How bad were you last night and how bad do you plan to be today? Tomato juice, 1-a, Clamato or V-8 are possible alternatives. As for pepper, Tabasco, horseradish, etc... use anything you've enjoyed as a marinade or spice for steak. If you're suffering, make them all suffer.

Variations

Bloody Bull: add beef bullion cubes.
Bloody Jose: use tequila instead of vodka.
Peppered Mary: Substitute pepper-flavored vodka
Mary Bleeding South of the Border: Substitute tequila for vodka

Law of the Land – Never order Bloody Marys or Ramos Fizzes in a busy bar after sundown.

BLOODY NOSE

1 shot Devotion Vodka   1 shot Irish cream
1 shot melon liqueur   Grenadine

Pour all ingredients into a shot glass and add a splash of grenadine.

BLOW JOB

1/3 shot Devotion Vodka   1/3 shot Irish Cream
1/3 shot coffee liqueur   1/3 shot Irish Cream
Float of whipped cream

In these difficult times, any job is welcome-whatever comes up. A wonderful thing to order in a busy bar, if you get a drink too bad. This invites some of the best responses you've ever heard. The funniest reply I heard came from Joe Zimmerman in Joe's American Bar in Boston, Massachusetts.

Customer: "Do you make Blow Jobs here?"
Joe Z: "Yes, we accept them as reward for good service."

Pour into a shaker glass. Shake and strain into a cordial glass. Float a layer of whipped cream on top and then - I hate to use the word- swallow in one gulp without using your hands. There is no substitute.

BLUE BALLS

1/2 shot Devotion Vodka *Splash triple sec*
1/2 shot blueberry schnapps *1 shot cranberry juice*

A very painful shot. Ladies, take our word for it. After some of these, people might think you're feeling the blues when actually you can't see or talk. Pour into a mixing glass. Shake, strain and pour into an up glass.

BLUE HAWAIIAN

1 shot Caribbean rum *Splash sweet & sour mix*
2 shots pineapple juice *1/2 shot blue curacao*

This is a tropical favorite. The color (not the taste) made it so popular. Reminds me of an old Elvis movie. Blend with crushed ice for a few seconds and garnish with a pineapple wedge.

BLUE LAGOON

1 shot Devotion Vodka　　　　*1/2 shot blue curacao*
1/2 shot sweet & sour mix

How many of you were excited by 15-year-old Brooke? You perverts! Shake ingredients in a glass of ice, strain into an up glass.

BLUE MOON

1/3 shot amaretto　　　　*1/3 shot Irish cream*
1/3 shot blue curacao

That's just the tidy bowl you're seeing with your head in the toilet. Layer in that order.

BLUE SHOTS

1/2 shot Devotion Vodka
1/2 shot blue curacao

Got this from the Hidden Shamrock in Chicago, Illinois. The taste is awful, but it sure is fun. Pour into a shaker glass. Shake and strain into an up glass.

BOCCE BALL

1/2 shot Devotion Vodka　　　　*1/2 shot pineapple juice*
1/2 shot amaretto　　　　*1/2 shot orange juice*

You'll be bouncing balls in no time. From Harlow's in Sacramento, California. Serve in a highball full of ice.

BOILER MAKER

Halfglass of beer
1 shot bourbon

You definitely have to be a bourbon fan, a beer fan, a Purdue fan and have a screw loose. Of course, there are those out there. Fill a shot glass with bourbon. Fill a pint glass halfway with beer. Drop the shot of bourbon, glass and all into the beer. Drink the whole thing. Check yourself into the hospital, then see a psychiatrist.

BOLSHOILEMONADE

(Bolshevik Lemonade)

1 shot citrus vodka   *1 shot sweet & sour mix*
1 slice lemon   *1 tsp. sugar*
Splash soda and splash 7-Up

Fill a highball with ice and add citrus vodka and sweet & sour mix. Add slice of lemon, sugar, and soda. Stir vigorously.

BRAIN ERASER

1/4 shot coffee liqueur   *1/4 shot Devotion Vodka*
1/4 shot amaretto   *1/4 shot club soda*

What the hell, nothing's permanent. If you're going to kill brain cells, it might as well be painless. Be sure to write down your address before you try this drink, so the taxi will know where to drop you. Pour into a highball with ice. Drink the cocktail as a shot using a straw. Say good-bye to all bodily functions.

BRAIN HEMORRHAGE

Dash of Irish cream
Splash of grenadine
1 shot of peach schnapps

Fun to make, fun to look at, hell to drink. I know it's made in many different ways, but does it actually start or stop the bleeding? Whatever means you use, the end result must be a shot that looks like an actual brain hemorrhage. My way is to splash grenadine into a shot glass. Pour in chilled peach schnapps, then, slowly tease in a dash of Irish cream, so that it collects in the middle of the shot to form a brain. To best observe a Brain Hemorrhage, look at your drinking partner. Unfortunately, you probably look the same.

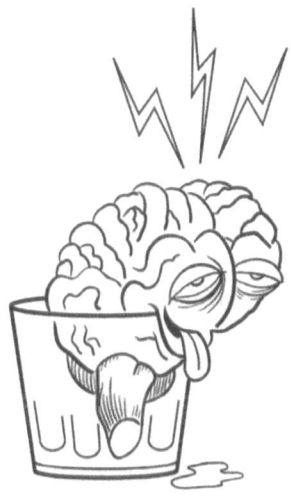

BRAIN TUMOR

1/2 shot peppermint schnapps
1/2 shot Irish cream
Dash of grenadine

Looks just like a brain in trouble-yours the morning after a big night. Your eyes are red, swollen shut, fluid oozing out your ears, all the blood vessels in your brain pulsating from the constant ringing and pounding, and it's your own fault. Pour Irish cream into a rocks glass full of ice. Add a dash of grenadine and let it seep down into the "brain." After a couple of these, you will welcome surgery.

BRANCH DAVIDIAN

1/2 shot Devotion Vodka
1/2 shot 151-proof rum
A lighter or book of matches

Shown to me at the Jerome Bar in Aspen. They have such a sense of humor there, those cult bartenders. Float the 151-proof on top of the vodka and light it on fire.

BRANDY ALEXANDER

1/2 shot brandy   *1 shot half & half*
1/2 shot dark creme de cocoa

Kind of like a chocolate milk shake, but you've never had a shake like this before. Packs a punch your Ovaltine never gave you. In a blender with ice, mix ingredients. Pour into a fiesta glass.

BROKEN HEART

1 shot Mount Gay   *1/2 shot triple sec*
1 shot cranberry juice   *Dash of grenadine*

A great way to heal, numb, and forget the pain (along with everything else). Shake and strain into a martini glass.

BROWN COW

1/4 shot dark creme de cocoa   *1/4 shot amaretto*
1 shot half & half

A nutty, foo-foo drink that'll provide you with your daily calcium. I got this drink recipe from Poor Reds in El Dorado, California. Blend ingredients and pour into fiesta glass.

BUBBLE BOMB

1 shot Three Olives Bubble Gum Vodka
1 glass of Red Bull

You'll be blowing bubbles all night. Out of both ends. Drop a shot of bubble gum vodka into f a glass of Red Bull and down in one.

BUBBLE GUM SHOT

1/3 shot peach schnapps   *1/3 shot creme de banana*
1/3 shot Devotion Vodka   *1/4 shot orange juice*
1/4 shot cranberry juice

Tastes just like bubble gum, but if you have too many you'll be blowing more than bubbles. Pour into a set up glass full of ice.

BURNT ALMOND

2/3 shot amaretto
1/3 shot dark creme de menthe 2 shots half & half

One a day, that's all we ask... one brain cell a day. Serve over ice in large rocks glass.

BUSHWACKER

1/2 shot Irish cream 1/2 shot Irish whiskey

Blend with ice until smooth, serve straight up. Is this sexually offensive, or what Clinton did in the last election?

BUSTED NUT

1/3 shot amaretto   *1/3 shot 151-proof Rum*
1/3 shot Caribbean Rum   *1 shot of milk*

It's painful just thinking about it. It was served to me at a bar called Scandals in Ocean City by a big, blond woman who made it in a coconut in her cleavage. I knew then that the drink was named correctly.

BUTTER BALL

1/2 shot butterscotch schnapps
1 shot half & half
1/2 shot Irish cream

You'll feel like a butter ball. I wouldn't call this the strongest shot ever invented or the smartest drink... unless you skipped desert. Pour schnapps over ice and float Irish cream on top, then float half & half.

BUTTERFLY

1/2 shot Devotion Vodka
1/2 shot butterscotch schnapps

"Float like a butterfly, sting like a bee," if you have more than one, don't blame me. Pour into a shaker cup. Shake and strain into an up glass. Watch out for the guys in the white jackets with the big nets.

BUTTERSCOTCH SUNDAE

1/2 shot amaretto
1/2 shot butterscotch schnapps 2 shots cream

Don't you ever just want to order a drink that'll really piss your bartender off? Well this is it. Serve over crushed ice in small rocks glass.

BUTTERY NIPPLE

1/2 shot Irish cream
1/2 shot butterscotch schnapps

I guess this takes the place of buttered buns with your eggs and sausage in the morning. Shaken and strained into a martini glass.

CACTUS COOLER

1 shot mandarin vodka   *Splash orange juice*
1/2 shot peach schnapps   *Splash pineapple juice*
1 shot Red Bull

Popular in Newport Beach, CA. It's a beach town and I didn't see any cactus there. Actually didn't see anything after a couple of these. Pour in a highball with ice.

CACTUS FLOWER

Shot of peppermint schnapps Splash of tequila

For the little prick in all of us. A sick combination, but I promise it tastes great. Add a little zest to the peppermint schnapps mouthwash. Found at the Pier St. Annex in Tahoe City, California. Pour ingredients into a shaker glass. Shake and strain into an up glass.

CAESAR COCKTAIL

1 shot Devotion Vodka   *Clamato cocktail*
Dash of Worcestershire   *Dash of Tabasco*
Salt &pepper

Shown to me by John Bandy, the man who trained Tom Cruise to bartend in the movie "Cocktail." Pour vodka and dashes of Worcestershire and Tabasco in a setup glass filled with ice, rimmed with salt. Fill glass with Clamato cocktail and shake. Garnish with a lime.

Caesar Cocktail

CAFE ROYAL

1 shot brandy
1 sugar cube
Coffee

A traditional, no nonsense caffeine/alcohol buzz. Stir in 1 cube of sugar in an Irish Coffee glass filled 1/2 of the way with coffee then add a shot of brandy.

CAIPARINHA

1 shot of Cachaca or Light Rum
2 tablespoons sugar or 1 shot simple syrup
1 Lime

The national drink of Brazil. This is what gives them that famous casual moral attitude. Lots of great things developed from Brazil after a few of these. The Brazilian wax is another that I can think of. In a shaker, muddle lime and sugar. Add Cachaca or Rum and ice and pour into a highball glass. Garnish with a lime.

CALIFORNIA COCKTAIL

1 shot of Devotion Vodka   *1 shot orange juice*
1 shot grapefruit juice

Oh, those crazy, health-nut Californians. This drink is also called a mistake, for those color-blind people who can't tell the different between orange juice and grapefruit juice and just add broth. Serve over ice in a highball. Perfect when the surfs up.

CALIFORNIA SHOT

1/2 shot Irish cream   *Coffee*
1/2 shot tequila

A couple of these and you'll be basking in California weather... rain or shine. Makes you immune to any California disease. Pour Irish cream and tequila into a shot glass, and a splash of hot coffee and top with whipped cream.

CAJUN COLA

1 shot Jägermeister   *Cola*

Enough of these and you'll be buried in the bayou. Pour Jägermeister over ice. Fill with cola. It's really not as bad as it sounds. (Yes it is.)

CAPE COD

1 shot Devotion Vodka
1 shot cranberry juice

A Cape Codder for those from the East Coast, either way it's a fancy name for a vodka cranberry with a lime garnish. The addition of lime was discovered on one of those rows of numerous bars along Cape Cod. The lime cuts the cranberry juice. Amazing how this caught on. In a highball, pour vodka, fill glass with cranberry juice and garnish with a lime squeeze.

CAPTAIN COSMO

1 shot Captain Morgan
Slash of cranberry juice, lime juice, and triple sec

Nothing like a drunk super hero. Shake and strain into a martini glass.

CARAMEL APPLE

1/3 shot sour apple schnapps
1/3 shot butterscotch schnapps
1/3 shot Devotion Vodka

Tastes just like those treats you get at the fair. Too many will create just as big a mess. Shake and strain in a martini glass.

CAR CRASH

1 shot tequila   *Splash grenadine*
1 shot pineapple   *Splash lime juice*

You'll feel like you just got in one, and it'll take the Jaws of Life (no, not a hickey) to rescue you. Serve on ice in a highball.

CARRIBEAN COOLER

1 shot of Caribbean Rum   *1/2 ripe banana*
1/2 scoop vanilla ice cream   *1/2 cup crushed ice*

The head rush you'll get is from the ice cream, but this will ease you into stronger concoctions. Blend all together until smooth and serve straight up in stemmed glassware.

CARRIBEAN RUM COOLER

1 shot Barbados Rum   *1/4 shot orange juice*
1/2 shot sweet & sour mix   *1/4 shot Cointreau*

A refreshing beach cocktail that tastes like your suntan lotion. From Moose McGillycuddy's in Honolulu. Pour into a shaker glass full of ice. Shake and pour into a fiesta glass and garnish with lime.

CARRIBO

1/3 shot light rum   *1/3 shot dark rum*
1/3 shot Barbados Rum   *Float 151-proof rum*
1 tsp. sugar

You'll love this. Pour light, medium and dark rums into ashaker glass. Shake, strain into up glass. Float a teaspoon of sugar, the 151, light it and drink. Talk about throwing gas on a fire.

CASANOVA

1 shot amaretto
1 shot orange liqueur
2 shots cream

This will turn anyone into Casanova, or so they will think! Serve over ice in small rocks glass.

CASEIN CUP

1 shot Devotion Protein Infused Vodka
1/2 shot Blackberry or Raspberry Liquor
Two wedges of Blood Orange, Two wedges of Lemon 5-6 Mint leaves.

Make sure to wear a cup. Add all ingredients in a tall Collins glass, muddle evenly pressing all juice out of the citrus.

CBA

1/2 shot brandy   *Splash coffee*
1/2 shot Anisette

One of these drinks that uses initials because they were too hammered to come up with a name. Pour ingredients into a rocks glass.

CC7

1 shot Canadian Club
1 shot 7-Up

I just love these number cocktails. You sound scientific when you order them, or like you have a stuttering problem. Serve in a highball over ice.

CELEBRATION

1 shot amaretto
4 shots champagne

The celebration is that you make it to the bathroom. A champagne hater's toast. Pour a shot of amaretto into a champagne flute. Fill with champagne.

CEMENT MIXER

3/4 shot Irish cream
1/4 shot lime juice

A rather disgusting, yet satisfying special effects cocktail, one that you'll only try once. Pour Irish cream in your mouth. Then pour the lime juice in your mouth and swish them until they coagulate. It's just like a cement mixing truck. Now either swallow or spit it out, depending on how much you love the person you're with.

CHAMPAGNE COCKTAIL

Glass of champagne
Dash of bitters
1 sugar cube

To help force down that cheap champagne at cheap weddings. Soak a sugar cube in bitters, then place it in a champagne flute and fill with champagne. Garnish with a twist.

CHAMPION'S CHAMPION

1 shot Devotion Vodka   *1 shot gin*
1 shot rum   *1 shot scotch*
1 shot bourbon   *1 shot Myers*
1 shot Chambord   *1 shot tripe sec*
1 shot pineapple juice   *1 shot orange juice*

From Champions in Georgetown, Washington, D.C., this was the big drink. You can only make rounds of ten with this, though it's obvious with all the junk in it. Fill (large) shaker glass with ice. Add everything. Pour 10 shots. You'll have nine new enemies.

CHASE AWAY THE COLD

1 shot amaretto
4 shots heated lemon juice

Have two of these and call me in the morning. Rim cup with sugar, pour shot of amaretto, fill glass with heated lemon juice, garnish with cinnamon stick.

CHEAP SUNGLASSES

2/3 shot Devotion Vodka
1/3 shot peach schnapps
1 shot grapefruit juice

A great name for a drink. What were they thinking of when they named it? Know how you're always losing your sunglasses? Best to buy them cheap and in mass quantities. Pour into a shaker glass. Shake and strain into an up glass.

CHEMICAL IMBALANCE

1/2 shot Jägermeister
1/2 shot Devotion Vodka

You'll loose all balance after one of these. (Also called a Slave Master). You'll wonder why you can't think straight. Chill ingredients and pour into shot glass.

CHERNOBYL

1/2 shot cinnamon schnapps
1/2 shot Devotion Vodka

This can also be called a Hot Russian; either way it's guaranteed to light you up and you won't feel the effects for a long time. Pour into a shaker glass. Shake, strain and pour into an up glass.

CHERRY BOMBS

1 shot 151 rum
Maraschino cherries

Great for a bedtime snack, that extra strong Manhattan, and also to put in your little troublemaker nephew's Shirley Temple. Soak cherries in the 151 rum overnight, then serve to the unknowing.

CHERRYBUSTER (SHOOTER)

1/2 bottle peppermint schnapps
Maraschino cherries

Makes your sheets look like a Japanese war flag. Fill glass of peppermint schnapps with Maraschino cherries. Chill overnight. Serve in a shot glass with cherry. Created by Buster Highman.

CHIP SHOT

3/4 oz. Irish cream Hot coffee
3/4 oz. Tuaca

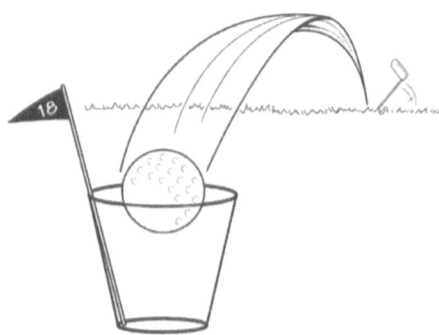

Great shot approaching the 19th hole. Mix Irish cream and Tuaca, add a splash of coffee, then serve in a shot glass.

CHOCOLATE CHIP COOKIE

1/2 shot dark creme de cocoa
1/2 shot Frangelico
1 shot half & half

Taste just like what mom used to make. Drink these cookies, then toss your cookies. Shake and serve in a highball.

CHOCOLATE HEIDI

1 shot peppermint schnapps
1 glass hot chocolate

Fill mug with hot chocolate, top with whipped cream and nutmeg. Be careful, this will go right to your thighs (I don't mean the drool). This one comes from a little Swiss chalet high up in the Alps.

CHOCOLATE MARTINI

1 shot Devotion Vodka
Splash of white creme de cocoa

A drink for the chocoholic-alcoholic! Pour ingredients into shaker glass, stir and strain into a martini glass. Tasty trick: slice a strawberry or maraschino cherry, and rub it around the rim of the martini glass, then dip the glass rim into chocolate cocoa powder.

CHRISTMAS PUNCH

1 bottle red wine
1/2 cup juice of a lime
3 cups English Tea

1/2 bottle dark rum
1/2 cup orange juice
2 T sugar

Makes a large quantity, so perfect for that holiday get togethers and leave togethers. Heat all ingredients, then, heat yourself. Use a saucepan for heating (the punch).

CITRUS LEMONADE

1 shot citrus vodka　　　*1 tsp. sugar*
2 slices fresh lemon　　　*7-Up*

From Bigsby's Bar & Grill in Chicago, Illinois. A refreshing, real lemonade cocktail. Quench that thirst and cool down, then fall down. In a pint glass full of ice, pour citrus vodka. Add lemon and sugar. Fill with 7-Up. Shake and serve.

CJ PARADISE

1 shot rum
Splash Chambord

From Corpus Christi, Texas... the paradise capital of the world? Pour into a set up glass with ice. Shake and strain into an up glass.

CLOCKWORK ORANGE

1/2 shot yellow chartreuse   1 drop orange flower water
1/2 shot tequila

Don't think you'll be doing any of "the old in and out" after this shot, because your own mechanism will be badly damaged. In a setup glass with ice, pour half shots of yellow (oh my God!) chartreuse and tequila. Add orange flower water. Stir with a muddler and strain into a shot glass. This shot is small but potent- you'll feel the "ultraviolence" being done to your brain.

CLOISTER

1/2 shot gin   1/2 shot tonic
1/2 shot Devotion Vodka   1/2 shot cranberry juice
Splash melon liqueur

What is a Cloister? What is this drink made of? Who drinks it? Mix together. Shake and strain in an up glass, and don't ask stupid questions. Have a couple, you'll know what it means.

CLOUDY MIST

1/2 shot Irish cream   *1/2 shot amaretto*
Hot coffee

I don't think you can see very well in this Cloudy Mist. Pour Irish cream and amaretto into a coffee mug. Fill with hot coffee and top with whipped cream. Great way to start the day.

CLOVER COOLER

1/3 shot Irish cream   *1/3 shot blue curacao*
1/3 shot Caribbean Rum   *4 oz. pineapple juice*
Club soda

The 4 leaves of the clover, but you're unlucky if you find this. Blend until smooth, serve in a tall glass with club soda.

COCKYDOODY

2/3 shot Jägermeister   *1/3 shot Irish cream*
Galliano

I wouldn't even want to try to think of a better name. In a shot glass, pour Jägermeister and Irish cream. Add Galliano and it becomes...too gross to name.

COCO CREAM

1 shot Irish cream
Hot chocolate

You'll go coconuts. Pour Irish cream into a coffee mug, fill with hot chocolate. Top with whipped cream.

COCONUT COLADA

1 shot Caribbean Rum *1 shot orange juice*
1 shot pineapple juice *1 shot coconut juice*
1/2 shot half & half

Perfect on the beach, in bed, in the hospital...wherever. Blend with crushed ice until frothy. Top with toasted coconut.

COLORADO BULL DOG

1/2 shot Devotion Vodka *1/2 shot Kahlua*
1 shot half & half *Splash of cola*

Sounds like a college mascot. Shake and strain the vodka, Kahlua, and half & half and pour into a pint glass, then add the cola.

COMFORTABLE SCREW

1/3 shot Devotion Vodka *1/3 shot orange juice*
1/3 shot Southern Comfort

As if there is an uncomfortable one. Serve with ice in a highball glass.

COMFY JAGY

1/2 shot Southern Comfort
1/2 shot Jägermeister

There really is no such thing as a Jager that is comfy, but what the heck. In a shot glass, pour Southern Comfort and Jägermeister.

CONTINENTAL

1 shot Hennessey   *1 splash Grand Marnier*
1 shot cranberry juice   *1 shot grapefruit juice*

You just won't know what continent you're on. Shake and strain ingredients into a martini glass.

COSMOPOLITAN

1 shot Devotion Vodka   *Splash of triple sec*
Splash of cranberry juice   *Splash of lime juice*

This sounds like a GQ, yuppie type of drink, but it's not. Don't let that pretty pink color fool you. This really packs a wallop and tastes good too. Pour into a shaker glass with ice. Shake, strain and serve in an up glass.

COW GIRL COCKSUCKER

1/3 shot Devotion Vodka   *1/3 shot Irish cream*
1/3 shot butterscotch schnapps

Please, don't blame me for putting this name in the book. I got this recipe from two pretty young gals when I was in Scottsdale, Arizona for spring training at a local pub called Hops. They gave me another drink (see Stiff Dick) and then this new cocktail...so blame them for everything.

Pour into a shaker glass with ice. Shake and strain into an up glass. Top with whipped cream.

CRANAPPLE

1 shot Devotion Vodka   *1/2 shot cranberry juice*
1/2 shot apple schnapps

A refreshing cocktail. Perfect as a thirst quencher and great for that buzz. Pour vodka and apple schnapps into a highball. Fill glass (virtually a half shot) with cranberry juice.

CREAM N- PEACHES

1/2 shot Irish Cream   *Soda and cream*
1/2 shot peach schnapps

Isn't this top shelf yogurt? Serve over ice with a splash of cream and soda.

CREAM SICKLE

1/2 shot Grand Marnier *Splash half & half and OJ*
1/2 shot Galliano *Dash of grenadine*

Tastes just like your favorite pop sickle on a stick, and just as messy. Shake and strain into a martini glass.

CREAMY LIME FIZZ

1 shot lime juice *1 shot milk*
1 shot of gin *2 shots cream*
2 tsp. sugar *1 shot club soda*

Be careful, you'll look like Old Yeller before they shot him. Combine all ingredients with ice and shake. Strain into a tall glass filled with ice and top with club soda.

CRIMSON SOUR

1/2 shot Dewar's *3 shots of sweet & sour mix*
1/2 shot grenadine

This makes you feel like a college mascot. Shake or blend ingredients quickly with ice. Pour into a tall glass and garnish with orange wheel and Maraschino cherry.

CUBA LIBRA

1 shot rum
1 shot cola

A cool name for a rum and coke with a lime. Those tricky people. Serve on ice in a highball glass and garnish with a lime.

CUM IN A HOT TUB

1 shot peach schnapps   *1 drop half & half*
Splash of 151-proof rum

A favorite for those evening pool parties. Not many drinks evoke a reaction quite like this one. Everything from hysteria to total disgust, and I would say that when you finally see one, you'll see why only one out of five are actually consumed. Make sure you wash the glass when it's done. Pour 151 into a rocks glass. Add shot of peach schnapps. Drop one drop of half & half into the "hot tub." (An Orgy In a Hot Tub simply involves more cream.)

D

DAIQUIRI

1 shot rum   *Splash lime juice*
1 shot sweet & sour mix

The traditional daiquiri made before the idea of adding fresh fruit became popular. Shake ingredients and serve in a fiesta glass.

DAIQUIRI, FRESH FRUIT

1 shot rum
Scoop of sherbert flavored with matching flavor
Splash of orange juice, pineapple juice & cranberry juice

For those that love milk shakes and not the taste of alcohol, but do enjoy a slight buzz.

DEPTH CHARGE

1 shot 151-proof rum   *Half-pint of beer*

Stay away from this explosion. That's all I have to say. Pour 151 into a shot glass. Drop the shot, glass and all into a pint glass half-filled with beer. Drink. (For more fun, light the 151.)

DEVOTED BULL

The Bull is named for the pick up lines that'll be coming out your mouth after a few of these.

1 shot Devotion Protein Infused Vodka,
1 shot of Red Bull, Splash of Cranberry
Pour into a highball with ice.

DEVOTION POTION

1 shot of Devotion Vodka   *1/4 shot Peach Schnapps.*
1/4 shot Amaretto   *Orange Juice and Cranberry Juice*

Isn't that called a Micky? Pour into a Pint glass with ice. Garnish with an orange slice.

DEVOTION PRESS

1 shot Devotion Protein Infused Vodka   *squeeze of lime*
1 shot of Soda and 7up   *Pour into a highball.*

For those with relationship issues. Fill with equal parts of Soda and 7up. Add a squeeze of Lime.

DEXTER

1 shot Devotion Vodka 1 shot cola

This could be called anything, but the first person who ever ordered this from me called it this, so this name goes to you. Pour a shot of vodka and cola into a highball full of ice.

DEXTER PLUS

1/2 shot Devotion Vodka   *1/2 shot Jägermeister*
1 shot cola

The guys who started drinking these ordered four at a time! I wanted to cut them off and throw them out when they told me what to put in them, but I felt sorry for them. Serve in a highball over ice. Don't blame me for anything that happens next.

DINGLE BERRY

2/3 shot Jägermeister   *1/3 shot apple schnapps*
Splash cranberry juice

DIRTY HARRY

1/2 shot Grand Marnier 1/2 shot Tia Maria

This will definitely make your day. Serve on ice in a rocks glass.

DIRTY MOTHER

1/2 shot brandy
1/2 shot coffee liqueur

Oh, Mom. You hate to think that some of the older, crazier ladies are actually mothers, or that your own mother does what they do. Serve over ice in rocks glass.

DI SARONNO COOLER

1 shot amaretto
2 shots cranberry juice
3 shots orange juice soda

Perfect for by the pool drinking binges. Can also be used as a great sunscreen. Serve over ice in large rocks glass with a splash of soda.

DI SARONNO DREAMSICLE

1 shot of amaretto
2 shots orange juice 3 shots cream

Not a big buzz, but will cause a big waistline. Blend to milkshake consistency. Serve in a large wine or balloon glass.

DI SARONNO SHORTCAKE

1/2 shot amaretto   *1/2 shot Tuaca*
2 oz. strawberries   *3 shots cream*

I just have to warn you, your bartender will hate you. Blend to milkshake consistency.

DI SARONNO SURFER

1/2 shot amaretto
1/2 shot Carribean Rum
1 shot cranberry juice
1 shot pineapple juice

Sounds like drooling surfers. Help you catch that perfect wave (in your waterbed). Serve over ice in a tall Collins glass.

DISARITA

1 shot amaretto
1 shot tequila
2 shots sweet & sour mix
1 shot lime juice
1/2 shot triple sec
Lime wedges

Makes you dyslexic, senorita. Pour ingredients into a highball full of ice. Adios amigo!

DOG FART

1 shot 151-proof rum Dash of A-1 steak sauce

You'll never eat steak or look at your dog the same again. Pour 151 into a shot glass. Add A-1 and whet your whistle.

DOGFIGHT

1/2 shot Devotion Vodka
1/3 shot Baileys Original
Irish Cream
Splash lime juice

1/3 shot Grand Marnier
1/3 shot coffee liqueur
Splash triple sec

It's a Kamikaze versus a B-52. That's the real dogfight! It was given to me by a member of the New Jersey Air National Guard, 108ARW. Pour all ingredients in shaker glass full of ice. Shake, strain into an up glass.

DOWNHILL RACER

1/2 shot amaretto
1/2 shot rum

3 shots pineapple juice

Sounds like something going down your leg. Serve in large rocks glass.

DRAM-SLAM

1/2 shot Jägermeister 1/2 shot Drambui

Dram-Slam, thank you ma'am. It lasts about as long. Pour ingredients into shot glass and slam it down.

DREAM SICKLE

1 shot amaretto
1/2 shot orange juice

1/2 shot half & half

Kind of like a funky version of a pop sickle. Serve on ice in a highball.

DR. PEPPER

1 shot amaretto   *Half pint of beer*

This is a fun shot. Fill a shot glass with amaretto. Fill a pint glass half way with your favorite beer. Drop the shot of amaretto into the glass of beer and chug the whole thing down. Now, wasn't that fun?

DR. PEPPER FROM HELL

1/2 shot amaretto   *1/2 shot 151-proof rum*
Pintglass filled halfway from hell

This is for those who love beer, want that buzz and want it now. Fill a shot glass half with amaretto and half with 151. Fill a pint glass halfway with beer. Drop the shot glass into the pint of beer and chug away. For added fun, light the shot before dropping it into the beer.

DUCK FART

1/2 shot Irish cream   *1/2 shot Tennessee sour mash whiskey*

My God, who named this?
Someone who spends a lot of time in ponds.

DUG OUT

1/3 shot Irish cream　　　*1/3 shot peach schnapps*
1/3 shot tequila　　　*Whipped cream*

A layered drink with a kick. In a tulip glass, layer Irish cream, chilled peach schnapps and tequila. Float whipped cream on top, and get back out on the playing field.

DUNHAM GOOD

2/3 shot cinnamon schnapps
1/3 shot amaretto

What Madonna says after each conquest. Pour ingredients into shot glass and do it good.

EGG NOG

6 ounces cognac　　　*3 ounces dark creme de cocoa*
3 ounces dark rum

The traditional holiday punch, with a punch. Is nog really a word? Use 32 ounces of Egg Nog. Combine ingredients in a large punch bowl or pitcher.

ELECTRIC ICED TEA

1/2 shot Devotion Vodka, gin, rum, tequila, and triple sec Splash lime juice, blue curacao and 7-Up

Basically a Long Island with blue curacao and 7-Up instead of Coke and triple sec. Shake ingredients and serve in a Set up glass.

ELECTRIC LEMONADE

1/2 shot Devotion Vodka
1 & 1/2 shot sweet & sour mix
1/2 shot rum

1/2 shot tequila
1/2 shot gin Splash of triple sec

Basically a Long Island Iced Tea without the coke. So it's a little more of a tangy way to say goodbye. In a shaker glass, pour vodka, gin, tequila and rum. Splash triple sec and sweet & sour mix. Shake and pour into a set up glass.

EMERALD ISLE

1/2 shot Irish cream
Splash cream

1/2 shot brandy

You'll feel marooned in the morning. Serve over ice cream.

E.T.

1 shot Devotion Vodka   *1 shot Irish cream*
1 shot melon liqueur

You'll want to phone home after this shot. Layer in a tulip glass. Drink up and place that call.

EXXON VALDEZ

1/2 shot peppermint schnapps
1/2 shot coffee liqueur

Ruins your environment. You'll be spilling more than oil. Pour into a shaker glass full of ice. Shake, strain into an up glass then spill it on yourself.

49ERS FAITHFUL

1 shot Devotion Protein Infused Vodka　　　　　*Lime*
1 shot Soda and Cranberry

Great for Candlestick tailgates. Post game cocktail, halftime nibbler, or a —who *cares* about the game" heat on. Pour Devotion Vodka into a pint glass with ice. Fill with soda and Cranberry, Garnish with Lime.

HEY, BAR KEEPER!
GIMME ONE MORE
AN' I'LL GRANT YA
THREE WHISHESH . . .

FAIRY GODMOTHER

1/3 shot scotch　　　　　*1/3 shot amaretto*
1/3 shot Devotion Vodka

Don't be fooled by the name; she'll cast an evil spell on you, and turn your head into a pumpkin. Serve in a glass full of ice.

FERRARI

1/3 shot amaretto
2/3 shot dry vermouth

Red, pretty, fast and guaranteed to get you in trouble. Serve over ice in small rocks glass. Garnish with lemon twist.

50-50 BAR

1/2 shot Irish cream
1/2 shot coffee liqueur
Float of 151-proof rum

You have a 50-50 chance of making it out of the bar. Mix and serve as a shooter!

'57 CHEVY WITH HAWAIIAN PLATES

1/4 shot Devotion Vodka   *1/4 shot Grand Marnier*
1/4 shot pineapple juice   *1/4 shot amaretto*

This is one shot that tastes great and is good for you (gets you loaded quickly). I don't know how the name came into being, but have one and you won't care. Pour into a shaker glass full of ice. Shake, strain into an up glass.

Variations:

California Plates: Use orange juice instead of pineapple juice.
Florida Plates: Substitute grapefruit juice.
Massachusetts Plates: Substitute cranberry juice.
New York City Plates or *State of Washington Plates*:
Substitute apple juice.

FIRE AND ICE

1/2 shot peppermint schnapps 1/2 shot Devotion Vodka

Perfect if you really don't enjoy being sober. Serve in a small rocks glass over ice. Can also be used in your radiator.

FIRE BALL

1 shot Goldschlager Dash Tabasco

You'll have fireballs coming out of both ends. Serve in a shot glass, empty in the toilet.

FIRECRACKER

1 shot whiskey
1 shot cranberry juice

This will cause a small explosion in your brain. The taste is not as bad as you'd think, but then pain is. Serve in a highball over ice.

FLAMING GORILLA TIT

1/2 shot Sambuca   *Float 151-proof rum*
1/2 shot Irish cream

This will get you on that safari. Don't try it on yourself; we humans have too tender pink parts. I don't know who named this or why, but it makes me wonder who belongs in the zoo. In a shot glass, pour sambuca and Irish cream. Float layer of 151. Light, and shout. It only burns for a moment.

FLAMING JAGER

1 shot Jägermeister Splash Tabasco

Just makes your mouth water doesn't it. Pour ingredients into shot glass (but sign your credit card first and don't kiss your date after).

FLAMING RAINBOW

Layer of grenadine　　　　　　　*Float 151-proof rum*
Layer of white creme de cacao　　*Layer of blue curacao*

Dorothy never made this one. The rainbow will be in your underwear. In a tulip glass, layer grenadine, white creme de cacao, and blue curacao. Float 151 on top, and light it.

FLAMING SWEET JESUS

1/2 shot coffee liqueur　　　　*1/2 shot Southern Comfort*
Float 151-proof rum　　　　　*Flame source*

Experience the second coming. See God, Hopefully you'll be back on your feet in 3 days. In a tulip glass, layer ingredients with coffee liqueur on the bottom, then Southern Comfort and 151 on top. Set on fire. Send any complaints to the Boardwalk in Scottsdale, Arizona.

FLIRTINI

1 part champagne　　　　　*1 part pineapple juice*
1 part vodka

From —Sex in the City" - HBO TV. Mix in a pitcher and pour into champagne flutes. Then, throw a party on the rooftop!

FLU SHOT

1/3 shot tequila　　　　　*1/3 shot Sambuca*
1/3 shot 151-proof rum

This is guaranteed to get rid of the Irish flu. Pour ingredients into a shaker glass full of ice. Shake and strain unto an up glass. Drink and then quickly look for a garbage can.

FLYING DUTCHMAN

1 shot gin Dash triple sec

He's flying because of too many of these. Serve in a rocks glass.

FOG CUTTER

1/2 shot rum   *Splash of Bristol Cream Liqueur*
1/2 shot gin   *1/2 shot sweet & sour mix*
1/2 shot brandy   *Splash of orgeat*
1/2 shot orange juice

The fog won't go away until the alcohol wears off. In a fiesta glass full of ice, pour all ingredients. Serve in a bowl with dry ice.

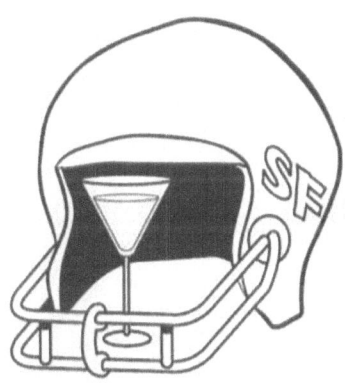

FORTY-NINER

1 shot of tequila
1 shot cranberry juice

The same colors as the '49ers. You have to be real faithful to drink this. Mix ingredients in a highball glass with ice.

FOUR HORSEMEN

1/4 shot Jägermeister   *1/4 shot Rumple Minze*
1/4 shot Goldschlager   *1/4 shot 151 rum*

I don't know who the mad man was who invented this, but if you don't like the taste, use it to clean your car engine. Serve in a shot glass.

"I put them on the Pope's bar tab."

FOUR WISE MEN

1/4 shot Jägermeister   *1/4 shot 151-proof rum*
1/4 shot   peppermint schnapps   *1/4 shot tequila*

You're not a wise man if you make yourself one of these. I guess the wise men are the ones who take your car keys, and the next day, tell you nothing bad happened to you worth remembering. Pour into a shot glass and kiss your short-term memory goodbye.

FREDDY FUDPUCKER

1 shot tequila Orange juice Splash of Galliano

I wonder how many of these the guy who named it had before this name came to him, or what he was trying to say anyway. Pour tequila into a highball full of ice, fill with orange juice except for a little room for a float of Galliano.

FRENCH KISS

1 shot of citrus vodka   *Squeeze of fresh lemon*
Splash of Chambord

A nice, moist, erotic cocktail that will sometimes lead to other cocktails (with nastier names). In a shaker glass, pour a shot of citrus vodka, chambord and lemon. Shake and strain into an up glass.

Passionate Kiss

Use passion fruit liqueur instead of Chambord.

FRENCH 75

Glass of champagne 1/2 shot brandy

Sounds like the name of a perfume. Tastes like one, too. Pour a glass of champagne and add brandy.

FRENCH TICKLER

1/2 shot cinnamon schnapps 1/2 shot orange liqueur

In case the other french tickler's not working.
Pour into shot glass. Drink and enjoy the inevitable.

FROM ANGELS

1 shot Devotion Vodka Float of Frangelico

You'll be seeing angels after a few of these. This is another of those shots for Vodka drinkers who hate the taste. Pour vodka into a shaker glass. Strain into an up glass. Float a layer of Frengelico on top. Drink, fall down, go to heaven.

FRUIT BASKET

4 shots of citrus vodka   *1 shot pineapple juice*
1 shot orange juice   *1 shot cranberry juice*
1 shot Chambord   *1 shot soda*

From Spanky's New York City. Makes four shots for 4 crazies. Turns you into a vegetable in no time. (Well, would you rather have it turn you into a fruit?) Into a large container full of ice, pour all ingredients. Shake and strain into four shot glasses for 4 people.

FRUIT LOOP SHOT

1 shot triple sec 1 shot milk

You won't believe it until you try it, but it tastes just like the milk after a bowl of fruit loop-and it's not just for mornings any more. In a rocks glass pour triple sec and milk.

FUNKY COLD MADINA

2/3 shot Devotion Vodka   *1/3 shot melon liqueur*
1 shot pineapple juice   *Splash cranberry juice*

A drink to rap to. Pour into a shaker glass. Shake and strain into an up glass.

FUNKY MONKEY

1 shot rum   *Half & half*
1 shot Kahlua

A couple of these and your monkey will definitely be feeling funky. Blend and serve in a Fiesta Glass. From the Blue Bay Village in Cancun, Mexico.

FUZZ BUSTER

1/2 shot Jägermeister 1/2 shot peach schnapps

Get's rid of all of your fuzz, except for the fuzz left in your brain. Pour into shaker glass with ice. Shake and strain into up glass.

FUZZY BEAR

1/2 shot dark rum   *1/2 shot orange juice*
1/2 shot peach schnapps   *1/2 shot cranberry juice*

You'll feel like cuddling everything in sight after this. Pour all ingredients into a shaker glass. Shake and strain into an up glass. Drink and cage yourself.

FUZZY NAVEL

1 shot peach schnapps   *Orange juice*

I don't know what they were drinking out of when this was invented, but what the hey. (It gets really hairy when you add vodka; see **Hairy Navel**.) Pour peach schnapps into a highball full of ice. Fill with orange juice. For better results, use body parts instead of glasses.

GALLION

1 shot of Caribbean Rum   *1/2 shot orange juice*
1/2 shot pineapple juice   *Splash grenadine*

From Red Robin (not the franchise) in Alaska. I'd never expect anyone to make suck a tropical drink in Alaska, but I guess it's perfect to sip in your igloo on a warm, sunny day. In a highball full of ice, pour Caribbean rum, orange juice, then pineapple juice. Splash grenadine on top.

GIBSON

1 shot gin   *Dash vermouth*

Basically a martini with an onion instead of an olive, and no, I don't know why they need a new name, it's just to make it more difficult for us. Shake and strain into a martini glass. Garnish with an onion.

GIMLET

1/4 shot lime juice   *3/4 shot gin*

Easy to order, easy to fall down. Stir with ice to chill. Strain into a cocktail glass and garnish with a line squeeze.

GIN FIZZ

1 shot gin   *1/2 shot lime juice*
1 tsp. sugar Club soda   *1/2 shot lemon juice*

Better than Alka Seltzer. Relieves all morning pains. Just don't plan anything that day. Mix gin, lemon juice, lime juice and sugar. Fill with club soda, shake with ice and strain.

GIN & TONIC (G & T)

1 shot gin   *Lime*
1 shot tonic

Easy to make, easy to drink, Fill highball with ice. Add gin and fill with tonic water. Squeeze lime into the cocktail.

GIN RICKEY

1 shot gin   *Splash lime juice*
1 shot soda

An old timer's favorite. A favorite during prohibition, maybe. Serve in a highball with ice and garnish with a lime.

GIRL SCOUT COOKIES

1/2 shot coffee liqueur   *1 shot half & half*
1/2 shot green creme de menthe

Who can refuse buying Girl Scout Cookies? They're for a good cause, but not yours. I wonder if they'll go selling these door-to-door. Pour into a shaker glass. Shake and strain into an up glass.

GODFATHER

2/3 shot scotch   1/3 shot amaretto

A deadly combination. Numbs your cheeks so you end up talking like Brando. Pour broth into a shot glass and pray.

GODMOTHER

2/3 shot Devotion Vodka 1/3 shot amaretto

This is what made them either wicked of a fairy. Serve on ice in a rocks glass.

Godmother

GOLD CADILLAC

1/2 shot Galliano
1/2 shot white creme de cacao
1 shot half & half blended

This is a foo-foo drink. Don't plan on getting a buzz from this, but it can help relieve that painful morning after. You'll think a Cadillac ran you over the night before. Mix all ingredients in blender. Pour into a Margarita glass.

GOLD FURNACE

1 shot cinnamon schnapps   *2 dashes of Tabasco*

This sure warms the room for you, and your pants. Causes sweating, heat strokes and convulsions. Pour into shot glass.

GOLD RUSH

1 shot cinnamon schnapps 1 shot tequila

From Gold Rush to Head Rush...to rush to the bathroom.
Pour into a shot glass. Drink quickly, you won't have a lot of time.

GOLDEN APPLE CIDER

1 shot cinnamon schnapps
Fill glass with apple cider

An apple a day keeps the doctor away, because you'll be hurting so bad you won't want to see anybody. Add cinnamon schnapps to apple cider and enjoy.

GOLDEN BEAR

1/3 shot Devotion Vodka   *1/3 shot coffee liqueur*
1/3 shot peppermint schnapps   *Whipped cream*

A delicacy from the Golden Bear in Oakland, California, near the campus of the California Golden Bears. This is one of those tasty shots that will soon get you completely obliterated and dancing on the bar. The hangovers are awful, but well worth it. Pour vodka, coffee liqueur and peppermint schnapps into shaker glass. Shake and strain into a shot glass and float a layer of whipped cream. Make sure to lick the whipped cream out of the glass after drinking the shot.

GOLDEN DREAM

1/3 shot Devotion Vodka   *1/3 shot Galliano*
1/3 shot rum   *1 shot orange juice*

Those are the best kinds of dreams, those golden ones, unless they're wet golden dreams. Pour into a highball. Fill with orange juice. Drink. Go to the bathroom before slipping on your jammies.

GOLDEN GATE

1 shot Devotion Protein Infused Vodka   *1/4 shot Melon Liquor*
1 shot of 7up and Orange Juice

You'll feel like you just jumped. Pour Devotion Vodka into a pint glass with ice. Fill with equal parts of 7up and Orange Juice. Float with Melon Liquor.

GOLDEN JOE

1 shot cinnamon schnapps
Fillglass with hot coffee or cappuccino

A cup of Joe never tasted so good, nor put you so fast asleep. Add Goldschlager to a cup of coffee or cappuccino and enjoy the warm fuzzy feeling.

GOOD & PLENTY

1/2 shot Anisette 1/2 shot Ouzo

Let's hope it's good because it'll be plenty, and your head will hurt plenty too. Pour into a shot glass.

GOOEY LOAD BLOWERS

2/3 shot Devotion Vodka   *1/3 shot peach schnapps*
1/2 shot cranberry juice   *Whipped cream*

Let's not talk about the name, who named it, or why. The only reason I included it is because people really do order it and, believe it or not, it does taste good. Pour vodka, peach schnapps and cranberry juice into a shaker glass. Shake and strain into a shot glass. Float a layer of whipped cream on top.

GOOMBAY SMASH

2/3 shot Caribbean Rum   *3 shots pineapple juice*
1/3 shot Australian Rum   *Lace with grenadine*

The two sounds you'll hear when you throw up and fall down. Serve over ice in tall glass and garnish with lime wedge.

ooopsie . . .

GORILLA FART

1 shot 151-proof rum
Dash of Worcestershire sauce

Ahhhh. Another mouth-watering name for a cocktail. And believe me, it is probably the best title this shot deserves. In a shot glass, pour 151, then add Worcestershire sauce Keep away from open flames and the city zoo and any small farm animals.

GRAPE NEHI

1/4 shot blue curacao   *1/4 shot 7-Up*
1/4 shot Chambord   *1/4 shot sweet & sour mix*
1/4 shot Devotion Vodka

This has been around for years, Sounds like an old favorite you had as a child, and will leave you acting like one. Pour into set up glass filled with ice. Shake, strain into an up glass.

GRAPE THING

2/3 shot Devotion Vodka   *1/3 shot Chambord*
1/2 shot sweet & sour mix

I don't know what the thing is, but if it looks like a grape... Pour into a set up glass filled with ice. Shake and strain into an up glass.

GRASSHOPPER

1/2 shot white creme de cacao   *1 shot half & half*
1/2 shot green creme de menthe

A minty cocktail, like a chocolate mint milk shake, without all those nagging mint pieces that get stuck between your teeth. Mix in a blender and pour into a fiesta glass.

GRAVI TEA

1 shot Devotion Protein Infused Vodka
1 shot Gin
1 shot Orange Juice
1 shot Rum
Splash of Grenadine

Named after Gravity in San Francisco. A couple and you really feel the gravity. Pour into a pint glass with ice. Fill with Orange Juice.

Shake to mix. Garnish with a Orange wedge and a cherry.

GREASY MICK

1/2 shot Irish cream 1/2 shot tequila

No offense here please. I'm just passing them on. Pour into a rocks glass and do what you like.

GREEK WATERMELON

1/2 shot amaretto
1 shot orange juice
1/2 shot Southern Comfort
Splash of Grenadine

This cocktail was brought back from the nightclub Mercedes in Athens, Greece. I don't remember much more of the vacation. Pour into a high-ball with ice.

GREEN APPLE

1/2 shot Devotion Vodka　　　*Splash of lime juice*
1/2 shot apple schnapps

Pucker up! It actually tastes like a sour apple. Guaranteed to turn your face green. Shake and strain into a martini glass.

GREEN BING

1 oz Devotion Vodka　　　*2 shots apple juice*
1/2 shot Midori

I don't know what the name means, but I'm sure it derives from the fact that after a couple your face turns green and your thing goes bing. Serve in a pint glass with ice.

GREEN FIRE

1/2 shot Ouzo
1/2 shot creme de menthe

This is not for everyone. Only for those whose taste buds have deteriorated over the years. Pour into a shaker glass full of ice. Shake, strain into a short glass.

GREEN IRISHMAN

1 shot Irish cream Creme de menthe
Coffee and whipped cream

How Irishmen look the next morning! This helps them on the road to recovery. Pour Irish cream and hot coffee into a coffee mug, then top with whipped cream. Drizzle creme de menthe over top.

GREEN LIZARD

1/2 shot green chartreuse 1/2 shot 151-proof rum

You know it must be tasty with a name like this. This shot crawled out of some primordial slop. One of these and I promise you'll soon be crawling on the floor, your tongue dangling in reptilian fashion. Pour into a shot glass and then go get a bucket.

GREEN SPIDER

1/2 shot Devotion Vodka
1/2 shot blue curacao

Makes you feel like they're crawling up your legs. Shake and strain into a martini glass.

GREMLIN

1/3 shot Devotion Vodka
1/3 shot rum

1/3 shot blue curacao
Splash orange juice

This makes you a mischievous, invisible being. Shake and strain into a martini glass.

GRENADE

1 shot Devotion Vodka
Splash Apple Liquor

Half a glass of Energy Drink

Named for the Jersey Shore term, and I've been the one jumping on a lot of these. Drop a shot of Devotion with a splash of Apple Liquor into half a glass of energy drink.

GREYHOUND

1 shot Devotion Vodka
Grapefruit juice

Another drink that has been around for as long as vodka has. A great drink for those dieters out there, and a great source of vitamin C. Pour vodka into a highball full of ice. Fill with fresh grapefruit juice.

GUILT FREE COCKTAIL

1 shot Devotion Protein Infused Vodka
1 shot Sugar Free Red Bull

Pour into a highball. Fill with Sugar Free Red Bull. The only thing you'll feel guilty about is what you do after a couple.

GUILT FREE MARTINI

1 shot Devotion Protein Infused Vodka
Hint of Dry Vermouth
Lemon Twist
Pour Devotion into a shaker glass with ice.

Add 2 drops of dry vermouth. Shake and strain into a martini glass. Garnish with a lemon twist.

Makes it so much easier to have just one more.

GUMMY BEAR

1/2 shot peach schnapps
1/2 shot raspberry liqueur
1 shot Red Bull
Splash of 7-Up

Sticks to your teeth, to your hands, your brain... Pour ingredients into a shaker glass of ice, shake and strain into a shot glass.

HAIRY NAVEL

1/2 shot Devotion Vodka   *1/2 shot peach schnapps*
Orange juice

Pour peach schnapps into a highball full of ice. Fill with orange juice. For better results, use body parts instead of glasses.

HAIRY NIPPLE

1/3 shot butterscotch schnapps   *1/3 shot Irish cream*
1/3 shot Devotion Vodka

An obvious hormone problem. It's also a side effect of the Buttery Nipple. Layer the Irish cream on the butterscotch schnapps, then layer the vodka on the Irish cream.

HANGOVER CURE

The perfect hangover cure, more alcohol. Here, the protein takes over.

1 shot Devotion Protein Infused Vodka Tomato
Juice and the Kitchen Sink

Pour Devotion Vodka into a pint glass.

Add a splash (to your taste) of Tobasco, Worchester Sauce, lemon juice, A-1 Stake Sauce, a dash of pepper. Fill with A-1 Tomato Juice. Shake vigorously, Garnish with a lemon and a celery stick.

HARBOR LIGHT

1/2 shot Metaxa
1/2 shot Galliano

Hopefully you'll find your house light, Pour into a set up glass full of ice, shake and strain into an up glass.

HARD DICK

1/2 shot Devotion Vodka   *1/2 shot Frangelico*
Splash soda water

Well, this is no longer a family bed side reading book. Shake and strain into a martini glass.

HARVEY WALLBANGER

1 shot Devotion Vodka   *Fill with orange juice*
Float of Galliano

This is a drink that will bring the house down. I don't know who wanted to put Galliano in a screwdriver, but a wallbanger comes to mind. Pour vodka into highball full of ice. Fill with orange juice. Layer a float of Galliano on top.

HAWAIIAN PUNCH

1/3 shot amaretto   *1/3 shot Devotion Vodka*
1/3 shot Southern Comfort   *1 shot pineapple juice*
1 shot orange juice   *1 shot lime juice*

How'd you like a Hawaiian Punch. Blammo! Down you go. Serve over ice in Poco Grande glass. Garnish with orange slice, cherry. Ouch, that hurt.

HEART THROB

1 shot rum

1/2 shot triple sec

1 shot orange juice

Dash of grenadine

Too many of these will cause a head throb. Shake and strain into a martini glass.

HEROIN

1/3 shot amaretto

1/3 shot tequila

1/3 shot Tennessee sour mash whiskey

From Obie's by the sea in Rehabeth Beach, Delaware. The effect is wild and it doesn't leave those nasty little marks on your arm. Pour ingredients into a shot glass.

HEAVEN CAN WAIT

3/4 glass champange

1/4 shot Devotion Vodka

1/4 shot orange juice

...*So* can your date. From Mark, the great cocktailer from New Orleans

HIBERNATOR

1/2 shot Barenjager

1/2 shot Devotion Vodka

Lights out! Good Night! See you when it wears off. Pour into shaker glass with ice, Shake and strain into up glass. Drink, see you in the spring.

HIGHBALL

1 shot of your favorite liquor
1 shot of either soda or water

Which name came first, the drink or the glass? Serve on ice in a high-ball glass. (Hence the name).

HIGHLAND SUMMER

1 shot scotch   *2 shots sweet & sour mix*
1 shot orange juice dash sugar

You'll be high, not know where to land, and get plenty of Vitamin C. Blend or shake with one cup crushed ice.

HONEY BEE

2/3 shot Devotion Vodka
1/3 shot Barenjager

This will only sting a little, and it'll keep you buzzing for a while. Pour into a pint glass full of ice, shake and strain into an up glass.

HONEY CHILD

1/3 Barenjager   *1/3 club soda*
1/3 orange juice

Causes baby talk, childlike behavior and stupid pick up lines. Pour into a tall glass with ice. You'll regress to childhood in no time at all.

HONEY NUT CHERRY-O

1/2 shot Barenjager   *Milk*
1/2 shot hazelnut liqueur

Mix Barenjager and hazelnut liqueur with milk. Breakfast of champions.

HONEY SUCKLE

1/2 shot Barenjager   *1/2 shot apple schnapps*
Soda water

Lip smackin' good. Pour over ice. It helps you get a honey to suckle...

HOPELESSLY DEVOTED

1 shot Devotion Protein Infused Vodka   *1/4 shot Pama Liquor*

Pour into a shaker glass with ice
Shake and strain into a Martini glass.
Garnish with a lemon twist.

You will be, to the person on the barstool next to you after a couple of these.

HORNY SHOT

1/4 shot Devotion Vodka   *1/4 shot Irish cream*
1/4 shot coffee liqueur   *Coffee*
1/4 shot Frangelico   *Whipped cream*

This will give you the urge to go looking for that special someone. (I know, all shots do that.) Fill an Irish Coffee glass 2/3 with coffee. Add vodka, Irish cream, Frangelico and coffee liqueur. Float a layer of whipped cream on top.

HOT ALMOND DELIGHT

1/3 shot amaretto   *1/3 shot Caribbean Rum*
1/3 shot dark creme de cocoa   *Hot coffee*

When your almonds are hot, it does make for a delightful evening. Pour amaretto, Caribbean Rum and creme de cocoa in a coffee mug, fill with hot coffee and top with whipped cream.

HOT BEACH SHOOTER

1/2 shot Caribbean Rum   *1/2 shot peach schnapps*
Splash hot coffee

Son of a beach is this shooter hot! Burns the bottom of your feet first. Mix and serve in a shooter glass.

HOT BUTTERED RUM

1 shot rum   *Cinnamon stick*
Hot cider and a pat of butter

Don't use pre-made mix unless you're lazy or just don't give a damn. Stir the butter into the hot cider. Add the rum and cinnamon stick. Have a few, then go back to that company Christmas party.

HOT IRISH NUT

1/2 shot Frangelico *1/2 shot Irish cream*
Coffee *Float of whipped cream*

I've been this way before, and boy is it fun to watch. In an Irish Coffee glass, pour Frangelico and Irish cream. Fill with coffee and float a layer of whipped cream.

HOT MILK PUNCH

3/4 shot Irish cream *1/4 shot cognac*
1/2 tsp. sugar *3 shots hot milk*
Dash of ground nutmeg

A great cure for insomniacs, but be careful of bedwetting. Combine Irish cream and cognac to dissolve sugar. Add hot milk and stir, then sprinkle with nutmeg.

HOT PANTS

2/3 shot tequila *1 shot grapefruit juice*
1/3 shot peppermint schnapps *1 splash of grenadine*

When your pants get too hot, you must remove them. But be careful about drinking too many — side effects can cause a dramatic increase in the temperature of the inside of your pants. Shake and strain ingre-dients into a Martini glass rimmed with sugar.

HOT SHOT

1 shot amaretto   *Splash of coffee*

Alcohol & caffeine... a great combo. This is the original "perk- me-up" shot. Not a big kick here but it does get you rolling when you have a long night ahead of you. Pour amaretto into a rocks glass and add a splash of coffee to it. Drink in one shot. Don't pour too much coffee or you'll have third degree burns from tongue to tonsils.

HOT TWAT

1 shot Tuaca   *Splash of coffee*

There goes any chance of a PG rating. Let's just get to the ingredients. Pour Tuaca into a rocks glass and add a splash of coffee. A great starter shot. You've got to try everything once.

HURRICANE

1/3 shot light rum   *1/3 shot dark rum*
1/3 Bacardi 151   *Dash of grenadine*
Splash lime juice, apricot brandy, sweet & sour mix

It'll be hard to walk and your head will feel like you're in the middle of one. Shake ingredients and pour into a fiesta glass. Float the dark rum on top.

I

ICED TEA

Mix iced tea with anything and everything. Great way to cool off, get wet, meet someone, warm up, get wetter... Fill highball with ice. Pour shot of your favorite liqueur. Fill glass with chilled tea, Add lemon, sugar, honey, or nothing... depending on your mood.

ILLEGAL ALIEN

1/2 shot Jägermeister   *1/2 shot tequila*

They'd rather go home than have to drink one of these. Pour ingredients into a shaker glass, shake and strain into shot glass.

INTIMATE ENCOUNTER

1/4 shot Caribbean Rum   *1/4 shot coffee liqueur*
1/4 shot Irish cream   *1 shot cream*
1/4 shot amaretto

Sounds like fun, just remember to respect me in the morning. Serve over ice in rocks glass.

INSTANT MILLIONAIRE

1/2 shot Devotion Vodka   *1 shot 7-Up*
1/2 shot light rum   *1/2 shot dark rum*
1/2 shot melon liqueur   *Lemon twist*
1 shot sweet & sour mix

Maybe you'll think you're one, and you'll be instantly anything else you want to be. Just hope you win the Lottery, especially to pay your tab. In a shaker glass filled with ice, pour vodka, melon liqueur, light and dark rum. Fill with sweet & sour mix and 7-Up. Shake and pour everything into a set up glass. Garnish with a lemon twist.

IRISH BANK

1/2 shot Irish cream   *1/2 shot Irish whiskey*

Named for the reason that to the Irish, alcohol is more important than money. Drop the shot in a glass of Guinness Beer.

IRISH COFFEE

Coffee
Layer of whipped cream

1 shot Irish whiskey
2 cubes of sugar

I had to add this because what a creation, coffee and booze in one glass; it contains your four basic food groups: alcohol, caffeine, sugar and dairy product. Developed and made popular at the Buena Vista in San Francisco. Now, these are very important instructions — this is for the perfect Irish Coffee. Heat a coffee glass; you must do this. Add one cube of sugar (two for those with a real sweet tooth) and fill the glass with coffee. Stir with a spoon until the sugar dissolves. Pour in a shot of Irish whiskey, then layer with cold real whipped cream using a spoon so the whipped cream doesn't sink into the coffee. Drink and you can be a wide-awake drunk person.

IRISH 49

1/2 shot Irish cream
1/2 shot Drambuie

Hot coffee

What does the 49 stand for? How many times you throw up? Pour Irish cream and Drambuie into a coffee mug, and then fill with hot coffee. Top with whipped cream.

IRISH KISS

2/3 shot Irish cream
Coffee
Creme de menthe

1/3 shot Irish Whiskey
Whipped cream

For those coffee drinkers who want to hide the taste of whiskey. This will keep you awake at night and your breath fresh the whole time. In a coffee glass, pour Irish cream, Irish Whiskey and fill with coffee. Float whipped cream and creme de menthe on top.

IRISH SOMBRERO

1/2 Irish Whiskey   *1 glass of coffee*
1/2 shot Tequila

Boy, that's all we need, 2 nationalities with cocktailing tendencies, loaded with caffine. Pour ingredients in a glass, float of cold whipped cream.

ISLAND ALEXANDER

1 shot Kahula   *1 shot dark rum*
1 shot Creme de Cacoa   *1 shot heavy cream*
Nutmeg

Yummy in the tummy, then fuzzy in the head! The editor's favorite cocktail of the Caribbean. Linda Roberts sipped Island Alexanders at the Simpson Bay Yacht Club in St. Maarten. Invented by John Jackson, the owner of the Saratoga Restaurant in St. Maarten.

ISLAND GLOW

1/2 shot Caribbean Rum　　*1/2 shot Devotion Vodka*
3 shots pineapple juice　　*Splash of orange juice*

You'll glow all night; you won't have to leave the lights on. Especially if your island has no lights. Serve over ice in rocks glass.

ITALIAN BANANA

1 shot amaretto　　*1 shot coconut juice*
2 shots pineapple juice　　*1/2 ripe banana*

Blend with ice until milkshake consistency.

ITALIAN KISS

1 shot amaretto
Mug hot coffee

Better than a French kiss. Sloppier? More tongue involvement? Maybe here you just skip the kissing. Mix amaretto and hot coffee. Top with whipped cream and chocolate sprinkles.

ITALIAN SURFER

1/2 shot amaretto	*1/2 shot Malibu*
1/2 shot pineapple juice	*1/2 shot cranberry juice*

Surf's up! Who needs waves? In a shaker glass with ice, add ingredients. Shake and strain into an up glass.

J

JACK MY JAGER

1/2 shot Jägermeister   *1/2 shot Jack Daniels*

You will be "jacking" a lot of things after a couple of these! Pour ingredients into a shot glass.

JACK OFF

2/3 shot Jack Daniels   *1/3 shot Irish cream*

This is something you drink by yourself...when you *are* lonely... when there's nobody else to drink with you. You get the idea. Shake and strain into a rocks glass.

JACK ROSE

1 shot apple brandy   *Dash of grenadine*
Splash of lime juice

Looks like a rose color, and I guess it would taste like one if you know what a rose tastes like. Shake and strain into a martini glass.

JACKSONVILLE STATE PRISON NOSE DIVE

1 shot tequila
1 shot grapefruit juice

1 shot Devotion Vodka
Salt

I will never understand why anybody would drink this, but prepare for your nose dive if you do. This is a tricky one to make. First salt the rim of a set up glass. In a shaker cup full of ice, pour vodka, Grapefruit juice. Drop a shot glass full of tequila into the glass, being careful not to mix the vodka with the tequila. Drink and go directly to jail.

JAGER BOMB

1 shot of Jägermeister
1 glass of Red Bull

You'll be dropping a bomb in the restroom after a few of these. Drop a shot of Jager into a half glass of Red Bull and chug.

JAGER BUCA

1/2 shot Jägermeister   *1/2 shot Sambuca*

I feel sorry for you right now. Good luck and have a safe landing. Pour ingredients into a shot glass.

JAGER CHOICE

1 shot Jägermeister   *2/3 part orange juice*
1/3 part club soda

Go pro-choice, because this is definitely not pro-life! Pour ingredients into highball with ice.

JAGER JIGGLE

Make fruit flavored gelatin as per directions, substituting one part Jägermeister for one part cold water. These are great for food fights, just don't get any on your skin!

JAGER MONSTER

1 shot Jägermeister   *1 dash grenadine*
Orange juice

Aren't all Jager drinkers monsters? As well as Jager drinks? Pour ingredients into tall glass with ice.

JAGER SEVEN

1 shot Jägermeister in glass of 7-Up

Oh boy, just your lucky number!

JAGER SHAKE

1/2 oz. Jägermeister
1/2 oz. creme de cocoa Milk or half & half

Great to order, this brings back the old line: "Hey honey, how about a Jager with that shake... Women bartenders love it, so do the big bouncers standing next to them!" Shake Jägermeister and creme de cocoa with ice. Fill with milk or half & half.

JAGER TONIC

1 shot Jägermeister tonic

Anything to crack that smooth Jager taste! Pour over ice and garnish with lime.

JAGER VACATION

1/2 shot Jägermeister   *1/4 shot Caribbean Rum*
1/4 shot dark rum   *1/2 shot pineapple juice*

You'll need a vacation after this Vacation. In a set up glass full of ice, pour all ingredients. Shake, strain and serve in an up glass.

JAGERNUT

1/2 shot Jägermeister   *Milk or half & half*
1/2 shot amaretto

You have to be a Jagernut to drink this! Pour into rocks glass. Your nuts will Jager in no time.

JAGGED SENORITA

1/2 shot Jägermeister   *1/2 shot tequila*

This senorita really is jagged. When you give this drink to others, never tell them what's in it because they wouldn't drink it, and probably wouldn't want to know anyway. Pour chilled Jager and tequila into a shot glass. Drink and say goodbye. (Actually, you might want to say goodbye before you have that drink.)

JAMAICAN COFFEE

1/2 shot rum   *Coffee*
1/2 shot Tia Maria liqueur   *Float of whipped cream*

For those wishing to experience the flavor of Jamaica without the jet lag. Pour rum and Tia Maria into an Irish Coffee glass and fill with coffee. Float a layer of whipped cream.

JAMAICAN SUNRISE

1/2 shot Caribbean Rim   *1/2 shot light rum*
1/4 shot creme de cocoa   *Splash grenadine*

To a pint glass full of ice, add Caribbean Rum, light run and creme de cocoa. Shake and strain into an up glass, and splash the shot with grenadine. The red color floats through. Tastes and smells like suntan oil.

JAMAICAN VACATION

1/2 shot 151-proof rum   *1/2 shot dark rum*
1/2 shot 7-Up   *1/2 shot pineapple juice*

You'll need another vacation after this Vacation, but isn't that usually true after any quality time off? In a shaker glass, pour 151 and dark rum. Add pineapple and cranberry juice. Your head will be pounding louder than the surf.

JAVAMEISTER

1 shot Jägermeister   *Coffee or espresso*
Whipped cream

Add Jägermeister to steaming hot coffee or espresso. Top with whipped cream. What a way to start the morning and end the day- at the same time!

JELLO SHOT

Your favorite alcohol mixed with gelatin dessert and water. Let chill and harden. They're perfect for food fights, jelly sandwiches, lubrication (for your car silly), and anything else that comes to mind.

JELLY BEAN

1/2 shot Ouzo
1/2 shot blackberry brandy

Taste almost like the famous childhood treats, and you don't look as silly eating them. Serve in a shot glass.

JIANNA COCKTAIL

1 shot Devotion Vodka   *Splash cointreau*
Splash cranberry juice   *Shot of sweet & sour*

A North Beach special. You won't feel a thing, or where you're at when you wake up. Shake and strain into a sugar rimmed martini glass.

JOE COLLINS

1 shot scotch   *1 shot sweet & sour mix*
1/2 shot Jägermeister   *1/2 shot tequila*

They'd rather go home than have to drink one of these. Pour ingredients into a shaker glass, shake and strain into shot glass.

JOHN COLLINS

1 shot bourbon   *1 shot 7-Up*
1 shot sweet & sour mix

To me, the strongest of the Collins brothers, but I've always foundbourbon to be very debilitating. In a highball with ice, pour bourbon. Fill glass with sweet & sour mix and 7-Up. Garnish with a cherry and a slice of orange.

JOHNNIE COLA

1 shot Johnnie Walker Red
Cola

Pour over ice and fill with cola. Be careful of this Johnnie.

J W. ICED TEA

1 shot Johnnie Walker Red   *Cola*
1 and 1/2 shots sweet & sour mix

So refreshing. You'll be cool, comfortable, and unconscious in no time. Pour over ice and fill with cola. Garnish with lemon slice.

JOHNNIE WALKER PRESS

1 shot Johnnie Walker Red   *1/2 shot soda*
1/2 shot ginger ale

You'll be pressed against the ground. Serve over ice.

Johnnie Walker Press

JOHNNIE WALKER 7-UP

1 shot Johnnie Walker Red   *7-Up*
Lime wedge

Sobriety: never had it, never will. Combine in an ice-filled glass. Garnish with lime wedge.

JOHNNIE WALKER SOUR

1 shot Johnnie Walker Red   *1/2 shot lemon juice*
1 tsp sugar syrup

Sour scotch? Combine with ice, shake well and serve. I thought scotch couldn't go sour.

JOHNNIE SPLASH

1 shot Johnnie Walker Red   *Splash water*

The splash will be you in your johnnie. Pour Johnnie Walker Red over ice and add a splash of water.

JOHNNY WADD

1/2 shot Devotion Vodka   *1/2 shot orange juice*
1/4 shot peach schnapps   *1/2 shot cranberry juice*
1/4 shot Caribbean Rum

Given to me by my bartender/Navy recruiter who has a taste for shots. This one is good tasting and good for you, too. Remember, Betty Ford Wants YOU. Pour into a shaker glass. Shake and strain into an up glass.

JOLLY RANCHER

1/3 shot Devotion Vodka   *1/3 shot Midori*
1/3 shot peach schnapps

Tastes just like the candy, only the effects are more fun. Shake and strain into a martini glass.

JONESTOWN PUNCH

1 shot 151-proof rum   *Sugar*
Orange and lemon pieces

This is a truly tasteless drink and you'll only drink it once. It'll really knock you dead. Pour 151 into a large punchbowl filled with orange and lemon pieces and ice. Add a tablespoon of sugar for every half gallon serving. Then everybody takes turns pouring into glasses and toasting. Good night. This is not a drill, it's a loyalty test. Enjoy with friends.

JORDAN VICTORY COCKTAIL

1/3 shot Devotion Vodka *Splash melon liqueur*
1/3 shot gin *Splash sweet & sour mix*
1/3 shot rum *Splash cranberry juice*

Invented by bartender Jim Jordan at a party honoring his Dad, San Francisco Mayor Frank Jordan, on the night of his victory celebration. Pour into a shaker glass fill with ice. Shake and strain into an up glass.

JUGO DE NARANJA

1 shot tequila *Splash of Grand Marnier*
Splash of triple sec

A very hip way of saying "shot from Hell." I love drinks that hide the flavor of tequila. Some people love the buzz but hate the taste. Pour tequila in a shaker glass filled with ice. Add triple sec and Grand Marnier. Shake and strain into an up glass.

JUNGLE JUICE

1 shot Vodka *1 shot cranberry juice*
1 shot Rum *1 shot orange juice*
1/2 shot Triple Sec *1 shot pineapple juice*

Pour over ice into Collins glass. Garnish with an orange slice and a cherry. Club Med party cocktail to enjoy festivities.

JUMPER CABLES

1/3 shot Irish cream *1/3 shot rum*
1/3 shot amaretto *Hot coffee*

I kind of like this, yet I also like cold toilet seats. Pour Irish cream, amaretto and Caribbean Rum into a coffee mug and fill with hot coffee. Top with whipped cream.

KAMAMWANALECU

1 Shot Devotion Vodka   *Splash triple sec*
Splash pineapple juice   *Splash lime juice*

Basically a Kamimaze with a Hawaiian touch of pineapple juice. Today it's safer to be a Kamikaze pilot rather that to approach woman with this line. Pour into a shaker glass full of ice. Shake and strain into an up glass.

KAMIKAZE

1 shot Devotion Vodka   *Juice of 1 fresh lime*
Splash Cointreau

One of the most popular shots around. The above ingredients are preferred, but substituting triple sec for Cointreau (a much better tasting liqueur) and lime juice for the fresh squeezed lime are okay. Make sure only a splash of each is used with the vodka. More than a splash and you ruin the shot- tastes like extracts. You don't want to taste the other ingredients at all. They are added to flavor the vodka, not to add some disgusting taste to your mouth so that you can't breathe and a river of drool starts flowing down your chin. Pour into a shaker glass full of ice. Shake and strain into a shot glass, and good luck gettinghome.

Variation: try different liquor instead of vodka.

Upside-Down Kamikaze: For fun, pour the ingredients into the open mouth of an upside down victim.

Kamikaze

KENTUCKY COCKTAIL

1 shot bourbon
1 shot pineapple juice

The closest thing the people of Kentucky get to a tropical drink. Shake and strain into a martini glass.

KEY LIME PIE

1/2 shot Devotion Vodka   *1/2 shot white creme de cocoa*
1 shot half & half   *Splash of lime juice*

Supposed to taste just like the popular dessert that nobody knows how to make. Shake and strain into a fiesta glass.

KILLER BEE

1/2 shot Devotion Vodka   *Splash sweet & sour mix*
1/2 shot gin   *Splash 7-Up*

I got this at the High Camp Bar on mid-mountain Squaw Valley, CA. I had much more fun skiing the rest of the day after a few of these. Pour ingredients into a shaker glass with ice; shake and strain into an up glass.

KILLER BEE HIVE

1/2 shot Jägermeister   *1/2 shot Barenjager*

The attack has begun and you'll feel the sting in the morning! Pour over ice, shake and strain into shot glass.

KILLER KOOL-AID

1/3 shot amaretto   *1/3 shot Devotion Vodka*
1/3 melon liqueur   *1 shot cranberry juice*

This will bring back memories. It tastes just like the Kool-Aid you drank as a kid, but you'll enjoy this alot more. Too bad Mom wouldn't make this for you and your friends all those years ago. Pour into a mixer glass, shake and strain.

KING ALPHONSE

1 shot coffee liqueur   *1 shot half & half*

This is basically a coffee liqueur & cream, but the name is for those who want to sound important. Remember to drink with your pinky in the air. Pour into a highball full of ice. That's it. Be careful of all those nasty calories.

KIOKI COFFEE

2/3 shot coffee liqueur   *1/3 shot brandy*
Float whipped cream   *Coffee*

For those Irish coffee drinkers who don't like whiskey, or for those coffee drinkers who like booze. (What does Kioki mean? Sing along with your coffee). Pour coffee liqueur and brandy into irish coffee glass. Fill with coffee and float a layer of whipped cream on top.

KIR

1 glass of white wine
1 splash of creme de cassis

A sophisticated way to drink cheap white wine. Turns wine into punch. Serve in a wineglass and garnish with a twist.

KIR ROYAL

1 glass of champagne
1 splash of creme de cassis or Chambord

Same as above, but for cheap champagne. Serve in a champagne flute and garnish with a twist.

KISS AND TELL

1/3 shot Devotion Vodka   *1/3 shot peppermint schnapps*
1/3 shot white creme de cocoa   *1 shots cream or milk*

This is how rumors are started. Serve over ice in small rocks glass.

KOOL-AID

1 shot Devotion Vodka   *1/2 shot sweet & sour mix*
1/2 shot soda

Makes you feel like a kid again. Tastes just like a glass of Kool-Aid on a warm sunny day. Goofy Grape, Loudmouth Lime — what memories! Pour vodka into shaker glass full of ice. Add soda and sweet & sour mix. Shake and strain into an up glass.

KITCHEN SINK

1/2 shot amaretto   *1/2 shot Orange Curacao*
Splash orange juice, pineapple juice, 7-Up, and sweet & sour mix

I don't know if this was named because there's everything in it including the kitchen sink, or because when it makes you sick you're bound to clog the kitchen sink. Shake and strain into a martini glass.

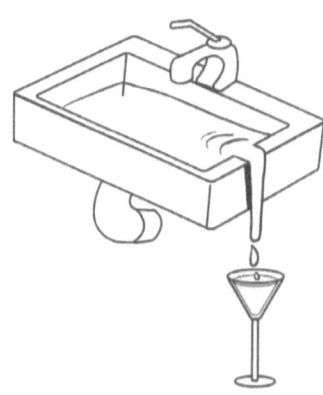

L

LEGGY BLONDE

1 shot Galliano   *1 shot half & half*
1 shot Devotion Vodka

I'm warning you, a date with this blonde could be dangerous. She'll mess with your head. Pour into a set up glass with ice. Shake and strain into a champagne flute.

LEG SPREADER

1 shot Grand Marnier   *1 shot hot water*
Lemon twist rubbed around the rim of a snifter

Well we can't promise that it'll work, but good luck. Heat a brandy snifter. Pour in Grand Marnier then hot water. This makes it easy to drink and hopefully her easy to... never mind. Don't drink too much though; the hangover on this could kill.

LEMON DROP

1 shot citrus vodka   *Sugar rimmed glass*
1 lemon dipped in sugar

Now this is on of those drinks everyone makes differently. I know of some people that add Galliano, some that squeeze lemons and add sugar. Some add 7-Up and sweet & sour mix. As far as I'm concerned, those are too wimpy. A shot's a shot, so why make it too easy. Plus, my way lets you have Citrus Vodka, a sugar coated rim, and you get to bite into a lemon dipped in sugar. And, most importantly, it's a heck of a lot easier to make when you're bartending and busy. Pour citrus vodka into a shaker glass. Shake and strain into a sugar- rimmed rocks glass. Do the shot, and then bite into a lemon dipped in sugar. You go rapidly from pain to relief to buzz. Just remember to visit your dentist.

LETHAL INJECTION

1/2 shot Malibu   *1/2 shot Captain Morgan's*
1/2 shot dark rum   *1/2 shot amaretto*
Splash of orange juice   *Splash of pineapple juice*

A great way to get rid of any trouble makers in the group. Shake and strain into a martini glass.

LICORICE STICK

1/2 shot Devotion Vodka   *1/2 shot Ouzo*
1/2 shot dark creme de cocoa   *1/2 shot triple sec*
1/2 shot dark creme de cocoa

Tastes just like the messy candy you had as a kid. And this is messy and makes you act like a kid. Shake and strain into a martini glass

LINCECUMAKAZEE

1 shot Devotion Protein Infused Vodka
Splash of Triple Sec and Raspberry Liquor

Named for the Giant's pitcher. Helps with your leg kick. Pour Devotion Vodka, a splash of Raspberry Liquor, Triple Sec into a shaker glass with ice. Shake and strain into a shot glass. Garnish with lime.

LIQUID COCAINE

1/2 shot Southern Comfort   *1/2 shot amaretto*
1/2 shot pineapple juice   *1/2 shot orange juice*

A very addicting cocktail. Have one and you'll do anything for another. And when you do, Liquid Cocaine Anonymous is there to help. In a highball full of ice, pour Southern Comfort and amaretto. Fill the glass with orange and pineapple juice. Drink, don't snort.

LIQUID HEROIN

1/3 shot Jägermeister   *1/3 shot Rumple Minze*
1/3 shot Goldschlager

So as to not get those nasty little track marks on your arm. Shake and strain into a rocks glass and enjoy the ride...to the hospital.

LOBOTOMY

1/3 shot Devotion Vodka   *1/3 shot Chambord*
1/3 shot amaretto

And this is no joke. Watch your friends after you sneak this in the punch at your next prom or reunion. Shake and strain into a rocks glass.

LOCAL ANESTHETIC

1/3 shot melon liqueur   *1/3 shot Devotion Vodka*
1/3 shot Irish cream

Local? My butt, I first tried this at Bacci in Salt Lake City and I don't
think it has worn off yet. Layer the ingredients in a tulip glass. Goes great
at mental hospitals.

LONG BEACH ICED TEA

1/2 shot Devotion Vodka   *1/2 shot gin*
1/2 shot rum   *1/2 shot tequila*
Dash triple sec   *Splash orange juice*
Splash cranberry juice

This is for those surfer types and those who can't handle a strong
taste of booze but want a heat on and want it fast. Popular in southern
California where they do a lot of things differently. In a set up glass full of
ice, pour vodka, gin, rum, and tequila. Add a splash of triple sec. Shake.
Fill with orange juice and cranberry juice. Garnish with lemon.

LOVABLE

1 shot Devotion Vodka   *1 shot Red Bull*

Makes you feel very lovable, and you won't care with who. Serve in a highball with ice.

LOVE AND DEVOTION

1 shot Devotion Protein Infused Vodka
1/4 shot of Raspberry Liquor

You'll feel this at 2am. Pour Devotion Vodka into a shaker glass with ice. Add a splash of Raspberry Liquor. Shake and strain into a Martini glass.

LOVE AND POTION

2/3 shot Devotion Vodka   *1/3 shot peach schnapps*
1/2 shot orange juice   *1/2 shot cranberry juice*
Splash pineapple juice   *Splash of 7-Up*
Splash sweet & sour mix

You'll be in love in no time... then you'll have to wake up and face reality. Just chew your arm off and crawl home. In a shot glass- not get ready- add vodka, schnapps, orange juice, cranberry juice, pineapple juice, sweet & sour mix and 7-Up. Shake and strain into an up glass.

LUBE JOB

1/2 shot Devotion Vodka   1/2 shot Irish cream

Sounds like something you have to do to your car, or your manhood. Pour into a rocks glass full of ice. Perfect for that after dinner drink before going on to wilder things.

LYNCHBURG LEMONADE

1 shot Jack Daniels   1/2 shot triple sec
1 shot 7-Up   1 shot sweet & sour mix

Where is Lynchburg, anyway? You don't want to be caught hanging around there. (Sorry about that-just had to.) This is one of the few drinks that actually hides the taste of bourbon. Pour Jack Daniel's into a highball filled with ice. Add triple sec, 7-Up and sweet and sour mix.

M

MACHO PUNCH

Clarence Demons, who not only plays a mean sax but is also a great bartender, gave me this recipe on a plane to London...guaranteed not to give you a hangover. In a punch bowl filled with ice, pour 2/3 of the way up with 3 rums: (1/3 light, 1/3 dark, 1/3 151), grenadine, sliced oranges, apples, lemons, limes... anything in your refrigerator. You won't taste the booze, won't know what hit you, and won't know what you did last night. No wonder the man can play so well.

MADRAS

1 shot Devotion Vodka *1 shot cranberry juice*
1 shot orange juice

A little twist to the plain old vodka-OJ. Get your Vitamin C from another source. Fill a highball with ice and add vodka. Fill glass half with orange juice and then half with cranberry juice. Change the proportions if you like, even add more vodka, what the hey.

MAFIA KISS

1/2 shot amaretto *2 shots pineapple juice*
1/2 shot peach schnapps *Splash grenadine*

The kiss of death Italian style. Looks good but they'll kill you. Fill a highball with ice, pour over ingredients. Splash grenadine on top

I WANT ONE OF THOSE!

MAI TAI

1 shot rum　　　　　　　*Splash triple sec*
Splash lime juice　　　　*Splash Orgeat*
Splash orange curacao　　*1 shot orange juice*
Splash cranberry juice　　*1 shot pineapple juice*
Float of dark rum

I love those Mai Tai's. You don't have to be in the South Pacific to enjoy them, because they'll give you a heat on no matter what latitude or time zone you're in. In a shaker glass, pour rum, triple sec, Orgeat, orange curacao, lime juice and cranberry juice. Fill the glass with orange juice and pineapple juice and shake. Pour into your desired Mai Tai glass. Float dark rum on top.

MALIBERRY

1 shot Malibu
1 shot cranberry juice

Can you get one of these in Mayberry? Serve over ice in rocks glass, garnish with a wedge of lime.

MALIBU BEACH

2/3 shot Malibu　　　　　　　*1 shots orange juice*
1/3 shot Devotion Vodka

Great way to cool off from those nasty fires and earthquakes. Serve ingredients over ice in a rocks glass.

MALIBU LAGOON

2/3 shot Malibu   *2 shots club soda*
1/3 shot blue curacao

This will turn body parts blue, and don't go #1 in public. Serve over crushed ice in large snifter. Garnish with orange slice and cherry.

MALIBU PARTY PUNCH

1.75 liter Malibu   *3 quarts cranberry juice*
3 12-oz. bottles lime juice   *3 liters seltzer*

The best way to get punch drunk without slapping on the gloves. Mix all ingredients in a large punch bowl. Serve well chilled with orange and lime slices as a garnish.

MALIBU SHAKE

2/3 shot Malibu   3 shots pineapple juice
1/3 shot white creme de menthe   2 shots cream

Blend with ice until smooth. You'll be feeling The Big One in California.

MALIBU SUNRISE

1 shot Malibu   1 tsp. grenadine
2 shots grapefruit juice

For you early risers, or for those who haven't gone to bed yet. Serve over ice in a tall glass.

MALIBU SUNSET

1 shot Malibu
1 shot pineapple juice
Splash of cream

Strawberries
2 shots orange juice

The sun will fall down, then so will you. Flash blend with ice, serve in rocks glass.

MALIMEISTER

1/2 shot Jägermeister   *1/2 shot Malibu*
Cola

For the cheater who can't take his Jager straight. Pour shots into a tall glass with ice. Fill with cola. Don't even ask who accidentally spilled these ingredients together and decided to name it.

MANHATTAN

6 parts bourbon
1 part sweet vermouth

This is another old time popular drink that too often too much sweet vermouth is added. A little more than a splash is all that is needed. Chill the bourbon and sweet vermouth, strain into a chilled up glass and don't forget the cherry.

Variations:

Perfect Manhattan: equal parts sweet and dry vermouth, garnish with a twist.
Dry Manhattan: dry vermouth, garnish with a twist
Rob Roy: use scotch instead of bourbon.
Downtown Manhattan: add a splash of bitters.

MARDI GRAS

1/3 shot Barenjager   *1/3 shot Chambord*
1/3 shot melon liqueur

If you find yourself naked in the streets celebrating, don't blame us!
Layer in shot glass.

MARGARITA

1 shot tequila   *1/2 shot triple sec*
1/2 shot sweet & sour mix   *Splash lime juice*
Salt the rim of a Fiesta Glass

A south of the border favorite. Drink of choice on Cinco de Mayo. This is just ingredients for a plain Margarita for those Margarita lovers (and there are lots of them). You can add sugar, or lime juice, or other ingredients that different bars use, but I'm just giving you the basic Margarita that will make you feel like you're back in Cabo or Cancun in no time. In a shaker glass full of ice, pour tequila, triple sec and sweet & sour mix. Add a splash of lime juice. Shake and pour into a salted fiesta glass, then run for the border (among other things).

Variations:

Cadillac Margarita: Top Shelf Margarita with a float of Grand Marnier.
Caribbean Rum Margarita: Use rum instead of tequila. **Electric Margarita**: Blue curacao instead of Triple Sec.
Florida Margarita: Add splash of OJ.
Fresh Fruit Margarita: Add your favorite fruit and blend.
Frozen Margarita: Blend ingredients.
Hawaiian Margarita: Add splash of pineapple juice.
Margarita Martini: Shake ingredients and strain into a martini glass.
Midori Margarita: Use Midori instead of lime juice.
Pink Margarita: Add cranberry juice.
Top Shelf Margarita: Use a premium tequila, fresh lime, and add Cointreau instead of triple sec.

Angel Martini
Asian Martini
Berry Berry Martini
Cinnamon Stick Martini
Citrus Martini
Coffee Martini
Cream Brulee Martini
Greek Martini
Muddy Martini
Sicilian Martini

MARTINI

1 shot gin   *Olive*
Touch of dry vermouth (one part to 8 parts gin)

The all too important Martini: To a Martini drinker, nothing is more important. What goes into making a perfect Martini is a question that will be argued as long as drinkers exist. First, a Martini is made with gin, I'm tired of receiving an order for a Martini, making it for the person, who tastes in and says he hates gin and wanted vodka. I want to kick him in the head. A real Martini is made with gin. A vodka Martini is made with vodka. Another misconception: you don't shake a Martini I don't know what James Bond is thinking, but a good Martini should be stirred. Shaking breaks up the ice too much, thus the gin becomes too watery. Stirring the Martini chills it more without watering it. But no matter what you do, make sure the glass is cold; chilled preferably.

Vermouth - probably the most disgusting tasting liquor when tasted alone, but oh boy when you add it to gin. Only a couple of drops should be added for the ultimate Martini. Although the ingredients says 8 to 1, the best Martini is made when you pour the gin while looking at the bottle of vermouth. For a great Martini, pour vermouth into a chilled glass, swirl it around, then dump the vermouth into the sink Chill the gin until cold, strain into a cold martini glass, and garnish with two olives.

Variations:

Angel Martini
1 shot Devotion Vodka Splash Frangelico

Asian Martini
1 shot Devotion Vodka
Splash Asian Dry Plum Wine
Garnish with a cherry.
Berry Berry Martini 1 shot Stoli Razberi Splash Chambord

Cinnamon Stick Martini 1 shot Stoli Zinamon
Splash cinnamon schnapps

Citrus Martini
1 shot Citrus Vodka Splash Sweet & Sour
Garnish with a twist of lemon.

Coffee Martini
shot Devotion Vodka Splash Kahlua
Garnish with 3 coffee beans.

Creme Brulee Martini 3/4 shot Devotion Vodka 1/4 shot Kahlua
Splash of half & half
- From Restaurant 230 in Laguna Beach, CA.

Greek Martini
1 shot Devotion Vodka Splash Ouzo

Muddy Martini
1 shot Devotion Vodka Splash Irish cream

Sicilian Martini
1 shot Devotion Vodka 1 shot Sambuca

Cajun Martini: use pepper gin or vodka.
Dirty Martini: add a splash of olive juice.
Gibson: garnish onion instead of olives.
Perfect Martini: sweet and dry vermouth.
Vodka Martini: use vodka instead of gin.

MATADORE

1 shot tequila   *Splash lime juice*
Splash triple sec

It's not the bull you'll be running from; it's what you wake up with in the morning. This is a Mexican Kamikaze. Here, use the triple sec and lime juice instead of Cointreau and lime because you won't know the difference. Pour ingredients into a shaker glass full of ice. Shake and strain and pour into an up glass.

MATZOH BALL 500

1 shot Devotion Vodka   *1 shot gin*
1/2 shot cranberry juice   *1/2 shot soda*
Splash melon liqueur

Sounds like a great race- a race to get hammered, then a race for the bathroom. In a shaker glass with ice, pour ingredients. Shake and strain into an up glass.

MAUI WOWIE

1/2 shot Caribbean Rum   *1/2 shot pineapple juice*
1/2 shot melon liqueur   *1/2 shot orange juice*

It's legal but just as lethal. Pour ingredients into a highball glass with ice. Promise you won't inhale.

MELON BALL

1/2 shot Devotion Vodka   *1 shot pineapple juice*
1/2 shot melon liqueur

This can be either a shot or cocktail, but since I like shots, that's what I'll describe. Pour into a shaker glass full of ice. Shake and strain into an up glass.

MENSTRUAL

1/2 shot Devotion Vodka   *Cranberry juice*
1/2 shot peach schnapps

You only drink these once a month (sorry about that). It sounds gross, but try it; it tastes kind of nice and real men aren't afraid of it.

Gets rid of that horrible PMS attitude. Any further comments will only ensure a quick slap in the face. Pour into a highball filled with ice. Close your eyes and enjoy.

MEXICAN COFFEE

1/3 shot tequila   *2/3 shot coffee liqueur*
Coffee   *Float whipped cream*

This is for those real sick coffee drinkers. You can adjust the proportion of tequila to coffee liqueur, depending on how far out there you are, or how far north of the border you find yourself. In an Irish coffee glass, pour tequila and coffee liqueur. Fill with coffee. Float a layer of whipped cream.

MEXICAN FLAG

1/3 shot creme de noyaux   *1/3 shot green chartreuse*
1/3 shot tequila

The colors of the flag. A couple of these and you'll be understanding Spanish and feeling like you ate Mexican food for weeks. Watch out — Motezuma's Revenge will hit you hard. Layer the colors of the Mexican Flag: creme de noyaux, green chartreuse and tequila.

MIAMI SLAM

2/3 shot Devotion Vodka   *1/3 shot blueberry schnapps*
1/2 shot sweet & sour mix   *1/2 shot 7-Up*

Courtesy of Mikey V, world-renowned bartender who invented this while at the Waterfront in Alameda, California. Very tasty, yet very poisonous to the system. You don't know the meaning of the word "slam" yet; but if you're in San Francisco, go see Mickey and just say "slam me" and hope for the best, Pour into shaker glass. Shake, strain into an up glass.

MIKOLOWSKI

Slice of lime   *Ground espresso*
Powdered sugar   *1 shot Grand Marnier*

A favorite at Pacific Heights Bar and Grill in San Francisco. Named for a Russian opera singer, this cocktail will loosen up the vocal chords while still allowing you complete control and range in your performance. Slice a round wedge of lime. On half of the wedge put a teaspoon of ground espresso, on the other half place a teaspoon of powered sugar. Make a sandwich by folding the lime slice in half. Pour Grand Marnier into a shot glass. Bite into the lime sandwich, chew off the lime pulp with sugar and espresso grounds, then shoot the shot of Grand Marnier. Just be prepared for the consequences of your actions.

MILK OF AMNESIA

1/2 shot Jägermeister
1/2 shot Irish cream

It does your mind good. Pour into shot glass, drink, try to remember anything, like why you did the shot, or what you did the night before.

WAIT A MINUTE...
IT'S COMING TO ME...
MY NAME IS...
...IS...
...IS...
...IS...

MILKY WAY

1/2 shot Kahlua   *1 shot half & half*
1/2 shot dark creme de cocoa

A couple of these and you'll be seeing stars... and floors, and toilets, and hospitals. Serve in a highball with ice. Everybody will get out of your way.

MIMOSA

1/2 glass of champagne   *Fill glass with orange juice*

Perfect for those Sunday morning hangovers. Better than aspirin to help ease out of that pain. Great to have in bars, restaurants, or just in bed if you can't make it out. Fill champagne glass with champagne and add orange juice.

MIND ERASER

1/2 shot coffee liqueur   *1 shot soda*
1/2 shot Devotion Vodka   *2 straws*

Goodbye. Call in sick right now, you won't be going anywhere tomorrow. Fill a highball with ice and pour in coffee liqueur. Layer vodka and soda. Serve with two straws, and insist the entire cocktail be downed in one drink. It is layered so you can taste the sweetness of the coffee liqueur first, cover the taste of the vodka, wash it all down with soda and go to sleep with the spins.

MINT JULEP

1 shot bourbon   *1 mint leaf*
Dash simple syrup

A tradition in the south to help ease down the medicine. Muddle the simple syrup and mint leave with crushed ice in a rocks glass. Add the bourbon and garnish with a fresh mint leave.

BOTTOMS UP,
Y'ALL!

MINZE JULEP

1/2 shot peppermint schnapps
1/2 shot bourbon

Mass Minzes means massive misery. Serve over crushed ice with a mint leaf. A poor man's mint julep; the lazy one's, too.

MISSIONARY

1 shot Devotion Vodka   *1/2 shot sweet & sour*
1/2 shot pineapple juice

I don't know if this instigates the position of missionary beliefs or belief of the missionary position. Shake and strain into a martini glass.

MOJITO

1 shot rum   *1 splash lime juice*
1 tsp sugar   *1 pinch mint leaves*
1 shot soda water

A couple of these and you'll be rafting back to Cuba. Muddle mint leaves, sugar, and lime juice in a Collins glass. Add crushed ice, then pour in the rum and soda. Stir and garnish with another mint leave.

MONGOOSE

A little of everything

Take the bar mat at the end of a busy night and hold over a shot glass. Drink whatever dribbles in. Perfect for that Final Final (and I mean final). Also makes cleanup a whole lot funner.

MORGASM

2/3 shot Devotion Vodka   Splash of triple sec
1/3 shot Malibu
1/3 shots of orange, pineapple, and cranberry juices

When you can't get enough of an orgasm. Shake and strain into a martini glass.

MORNING GLORY

2/3 glass of champagne *Splash of triple sec*
1/3 glass of orange juice

After a night of drinking, this could mean lots of things. Pour ingredients into a champagne flute

MUDSLIDE

1/3 shot Irish cream *1/3 shot Devotion Vodka*
1/3 shot coffee liqueur

A variation of the B-52, except a little stronger. The vodka gives it the much needed kick. Layer in a tulip glass. Then watch your mud start to slide.

MULTIPLE SCREAMING ORGASM

1/3 shot Devotion Vodka *1/3 shot Irish cream*
1/3 shot Kahlua

Of course this is a participation drink. First, lie the victim on the bar with their hands over their head. Put half a banana in their mouth. Put a pint glass between their legs and the tin cup sticking out the front of your pants. Pour ingredients into your tin cup and shake by gyrating your hips. Then pour ingredients, without using your hands, into the pint glass between the victim's legs, and take a bite out of the banana in their mouth.

Multiple Screaming Orgasm

N

NAZI FROM HELL

1/2 shot Jägermeister   *1/2 shot Rumple Minze*

This will make you remember all Nazis are from hell. One of the most potent shots but nobody ever remembers doing them, or why. Just remove objects from under all falling bodies beforehand. In a shot glass, pour Jager and peppermint schnapps. Drink and hope you don't get into too much trouble. Also called a Zebra or a Rumple Meister.

NEGRONI

1/3 shot gin   *1/3 shot Campari*
1/3 shot sweet vermouth

Pour ingredients into a shaker glass, stir and pour into shot glass. A classic drink that only hardened drinkers order.

NIKOLI

1 shot Devotion Vodka   *1 lemon rind*
Pinch coffee grounds   *Pinch sugar*

From Itrey Merii in New York City. A great buzz: caffeine, sugar, alcohol and Vitamin C. Cut a lemon rind and on half one side place a pinch of sugar. On the other half, same side, place a pinch of coffee grounds. Fill a shot glass with vodka. Drink the shot and chew the lemon, sugar, coffee ground combo. Don't try to justify your actions because it won't work.

NORI-JAGER

1 line of Sweet 'n Low   *1 shot Jägermeister*

Pour Jager into a shot glass. Snort the Sweet "n Low and down the Jager. I'm serious, and no substitutions for Sweet 'n Low either.

NUCLEAR FALLOUT

1/3 shot Jägermeister   *1/3 shot Irish cream*
1/3 shot amaretto

"The day after" never had it so bad. Pour ingredients into shot glass, and plan on radiation sickness.

NUT BAG

Don't even ask.

1 shot Devotion Protein Infused Vodka   *1/4 shot Frangelico*

Pour into a shaker glass with ice. Shake and strain into a Martini glass. I hope there's no taste comparison.

NUTS AND BUSH

1/2 shot Frangelico   *1/2 shot Bushmills*

What a team. They go so well together. Makes me just tingle all over. Fill a rocks glass with ice. Pour Frangelico and Irish Whiskey. Drink and feel sexually stimulated.

Variation

Castration: Irish whiskey straight.

Nuts and Bush

NUTS ON A NAVEL

1/2 shot Devotion Vodka   *1/2 shot peach schnapps*
1 shot orange juice   *Float of amaretto*

Starts as an inny, ends as an outy. Helps keep the lint out. Pour vodka and peach schnapps into a highball filled with ice. Fill with orange juice and amaretto on top.

NUTS AND BERRIES

1/2 shot Chambord   *1/2 shot Frangelico*
1 shot half & half

I first tasted this at The Boat House in Cambridge, Massachusetts.
I kept tasting it my whole vacation. Pour ingredients into a mixing glass with ice, shake and strain into an up glass.

NUTS N' HONEY

1/2 shot Barenjager   *1/2 shot amaretto*

What were you thinking? Nothin' honey... Pour ingredients into shaker glass with ice, Shake and strain into shot glass.

NUTTY IRISHCASE

1/3 shot Irish cream   *1/3 shot amaretto*
1/3 shot Irish Whiskey   *Hot coffee*

See author on St. Paddy's Day. Pour Irish cream, amaretto and Irish Whiskey in a coffee mug and fill with hot coffee. Top with whipped cream.

NUTTY IRISHMAN

1/2 shot Frangelico *1/2 shot Irish Whiskey*
1 shot half & half

Aren't they all? This is a very tasty dairy product that is guaranteed to get even the Irish plastered. In a highball filled with ice, pour Frangelico and Irish whiskey, fill with half & half.

NYMPHOMANIAC

1/2 shot Captain Morgan's *1/2 shot Malibu Rum*
1/2 shot peach schnapps

Now we're talking. I hope this works. Shake and strain into a martini glass. Make sure you save your energy.

OATMEAL COOKIE

1/3 shot Irish cream   *1/3 shot Goldschlager*
1/3 shot Kahlua

Don't have too many or it will become oatmeal pukie. Shake and strain into a martini glass.

"OH MY GOD"

1 shot Devotion Vodka
1/2 shots of cranberry, orange, pineapple, & grapefruit juice
1/3 shot apple, watermelon, and peach schnapps

You'll be seeing God. Shake and strain into 2 martini glasses.

OIL SLICK

1 shot peppermint schnapps   *Float Jägermeister*

Given to me by vacationers back from Bourbon Street in New Orleans. They didn't remember which bar they got it from, but they were coming from New Orleans, I'm surprised they remembered anything. Looks (and tastes) just like an oil slick.

OLD FASHIONED

1 shot bourbon   *Splash bitters*
1 sugar cube   *Orange slice*
Cherry

Here is a semi-secret way to make a fantastic Old Fashioned. First, you put a sugar cube, splash of bitters, the cherry and orange slice into a rocks glass. Mash them all together with your muddler and leave the mixture in. Fill the glass with ice and pour in the bourbon. Stir everything well, then serve. Old Fashioned drinkers love this technique much better than just serving the cherry and orange slice *as a garnish. These are for real drinkers, and it is the real drinkers you want to please.*

OOGY WA WA (AUTHENTIC ZULU TOAST)

1/2 shot amaretto   *1/2 shot peach schnapps*
1 shot cranberry juice   *1 shot grapefruit juice*

That's the way your wa-wa will feel. Serve over ice in a large rocks glass.

OOPSIE DOOPSIES

Mistakes you give away. Not a favorite of the management, but some customers will perch themselves right next to the well, praying these will come their way.

OPEN GRAVES

1/2 shot peppermint schnapps   *1/2 shot Jägermeister*
Splash of Irish cream

I know what you're thinking, these do not go together, but taste it-you'll just die. (I can't believe I said that.) But death will be refreshing. In a shot glass, pour chilled peppermint schnapps and chilled Jager into a shot glass. Then tickle a dash of Irish cream in the center of the shot glass. Call the undertaker.

ORANGE BLOSSOM

1 shot gin   *1 shot orange juice*

A way to get your vitamin C and kill your brain cells at once. Sounds like a scent for your bathroom. Drink too many and it will be the scent in your bathroom. Pour into a set up glass full of ice. Shake and strain into an up glass. Some like to add a teaspoon of sugar, but only for those who have a real sweet tooth.

ORANGE CRUSH

3/4 shot Devotion Vodka   *1 shot orange juice*
1/4 shot triple sec

This will squeeze the juice out of your head. And, it's not just for breakfast anymore. Combine ingredients over ice, add a splash of soda and garnish with an orange wheel.

ORGASM

1/3 shot Devotion Vodka   *1/3 shot Kahlua*
1/3 shot Irish cream

One of life's great pleasures. Serve on ice in a rocks glass.

OVERTURE

1/2 shot orange-flavored liqueur
Dry sparkling wine or champagne for topping up
1 orange peel spiral
1 dash orange bitters

Pour the liqueur and bitters into a champagne flute, top with sparkling wine or champagne, and garnish with orange peel spiral.

OYSTER SHOOTER

1 shot Devotion Vodka   *1 shot very spicy Bloody Mary mix*
1 raw oyster

You know what they say about oysters. But don't have too many or the mind will be willing but the flesh too weak. Plop an oyster in a rocks glass and pour a desired amount of vodka and spicy bloody mary mix. drink it and take a bite out of the oyster.

P

PARACHUTE

1/4 shot Devotion Vodka
1/4 shot amaretto
1/4 shot Tennessee sour mash whiskey

1/4 shot Southern Comfort
1/2 shot orange juice
1/2 shot cranberry juice

This will make that fall off the barstool as graceful and painless as possible. Or, if you're lucky, you'll only hear about the fall after it happens. In a set up glass full of ice, mix vodka, amaretto, Tennessee whiskey and Southern Comfort. Add orange juice and cranberry juice. Shake and strain into an up glass.

Variation:

Joe's Parachute: substitute shot with Yukon Jack (Canadian whiskey) for Tennessee whiskey, and instead of cranberry juice, add splashes of pineapple juice, grenadine and sloe gin.

PARALYZER

1/2 shot 151-proof rum
1/2 shot peppermint schnapps

The name says it all. Usually not permanent, but loss of feeling and movement should be expected. Should be consumed in the comfort of your own home-not recommended if you're on a date. In a shot glass, pour 151 and chilled peppermint schnapps. Don't forget the law of physics-that for every action there is an equal and opposite reaction.

Paralyzer

PARK AVENUE

1 shot gin   *Splash vermouth*
1/2 shot pineapple juice

A foo-foo martini or for those trying to hide their alcohol problems. Combine with ice and shake. Strain into an up glass.

PEACE IN IRELAND

1/2 shot Irish Mist   1/2 shot Irish cream

There's as much a chance for this as there is for the Irish to quit drinking. Shake and strain into a martini glass.

PEACHES & CREAM

1 shot peach schnapps   *s1 shot half & half*

This shot will do wonders for your complexion. Not bad on the taste buds, either. Serve in a highball over ice.

PEACH ON MALIBU BEACH

1 shot Caribbean Rum
1/2 shot peach schnapps
2 shots orange juice

There's nothing like rubbing your hand on the fuzz of a Malibu peach.
Serve over ice in rocks glass.

PEACHY KEEN

1/2 shot peach schnapps   *1/2 shot Devotion Vodka*

This will put you in that good-natured, nothing can bother you mood.
Pour into a shaker glass. Shake, strain and pour into an up glass.

PEANUT BUTTER CUP

2/3 shot Caribbean Rum　　*2 Tbs. creamy peanut butter*
2 Tbs. chocolate syrup　　*2 scoops vanilla ice cream*
1/3 shot Devotion Vodka

This drink will stick to the top of your mouth but unfortunately sink in your stomach. Blend all ingredients until smooth and frothy. Pour into fiesta glass.

PEARL HARBOR

2/3 shot Devotion Vodka　　*1 shot pineapple juice*
1/3 shot melon liqueur

Away to get bombed, but hope they don't remember what you did for infamy. In a set up glass full of ice, pour all ingredients. Shake and strain into an up glass.

PEARL NECKLACE

1 shot Devotion Vodka　　*1 shot half & half*

For when you can't afford one type and don't have the energy for the other type. Shake and strain into a martini glass.

PEPPERMINT PADDY

1/2 shot Rumple Minze　　*1 shot half & half*
1/2 shot dark creme de cocoa

Tastes just like that frozen cookie, and just as messy if you drink too many. Serve in a highball with ice.

PEAR MARTINI

1 shot pear vodka   *Splash grapefruit juice*

Delicious but not good for you. Probably not the most macho drink to order. I don't think many dive or biker bars will be able, or willing to make these. Pour into a shaker glass with ice. Shake and strain into a martini glass. Garnish with a pear slice.

Perfect Sex

PERFECT SEX

1/3 shot Devotion Vodka   *1/3 shot Frangelico*
1/3 shot Irish cream

Is there really such a thing? (Maybe if it came with a pizza and beer.) A couple of these shots could lead to the perfect thing, who knows. I'm usually by myself anyway. This is another one of those layered shots. In a cordial glass layer Frangelico, Irish cream and vodka. Do the shot and dream on.

PERSUADER

1/2 shot brandy   *1/2 shot amaretto*
Fill with orange juice

If this doesn't persuade her, give up. Why do people think that women need persuasion and men don't? I know, silly question. Just a thought. Pour brandy and amaretto into a highball over ice. Fill with orange juice.

PHILIPPINE BLOW JOB

1/3 shot coffee liqueur   *1/3 shot Devotion Vodka*
1/3 shot scotch whiskey

Who comes up with these? I don't know why or how this name was developed, so I'll just tell you how to make it. Pour all ingredients into a set up glass. Shake and strain into an up glass.

PHILIPPINE SLAMMER

1/3 shot Devotion Vodka   *1/3 shot amaretto*
1/3 shot Southern Comfort   *1/3 shot orange juice*
Splash grenadine

Boy, this is further south than the Alabama Slammer, and out there. Pour into a set up glass full of ice. Shake, strain and serve in an up glass.

PHOENIX

1 shot tequila   *1 shot cranberry juice*
1 shot soda   *Squeeze of lime*

A wonderful cocktail to refresh you, ease you into those warm summer days, cause you to lose all motor and visual functions. Oh well, what else are those warm summer days for? Fill a highball with ice and add ingredients. Garnish with a lime.

PICON PUNCH

1 shot Picon   *Float of brandy*
1 shot soda

An old, traditional cocktail that few bartenders under the age of 50 will know how to make (and, of course, not a customer under the age of 50 will care). Serve on ice in an Irish Coffee glass.

PINA COLADA

1 shot rum   *2 shots pineapple juice*
1/2 shot coconut syrup concentrate

A very refreshing cocktail for when you're in one of those tropical moods. Just don't order it in the Continental U.S. Mix ingredients in blender and pour into a fiesta glass. For added pleasure add a scoop of pineapple or coconut sorbet or vanilla ice cream.

Variations:

Malibu Caribbean Rum: Use instead of rum.
Melon Colada: Use midori instead of rum.
Italian Colada: Amaretto instead of rum.
Virgin Colada: Virgin means no alcohol and no nookie.
Orange Colada: Triple sec and Caribbean Rum.

PINEAPPLE BOMB

1/2 shot rum
1 shot pineapple juice
1/2 shot peach schnapps
Splash 7-Up

This is a bomb all right. You'd be better off banging a pineapple against your head. A great tasting tropical type shot that's let you feel the explosion for quite a while. Pour into a set up glass full of ice. Shake and strain into an up glass.

PINK CADILLAC

1/2 shot Galliano
1/2 shot half & half
Dash soda
1/2 shot creme de cacao
Dash grenadine

This is a Gold Cadillac with grenadine. Mix in a blender and pour into a Margarita glass.

PINK CLOUD

1/2 shot amaretto   *Dash half & half*
1/2 shot white creme de cacao *Dash grenadine*

There's no rain in this cloud. A foo-foo drink. In a blender with a scoop of ice, pour amaretto and white creme de cacao. Add grenadine and half & half. Blend and pour into a Margarita glass.

PINK LADY

1 shot gin   *Dash of grenadine*
1 shot half & half

Sure beats seeing pink elephants, and more fun to play with. Shake with ice and strain into a martini glass.

PINK LEMONADE

1 shot citrus vodka   *1/3 shot cranberry juice*
2/3 shot sweet & sour mix *Splash 7-Up*

A very tangy shot with a wallop. Just like grandma used to make. Pour into a set up glass with ice. Shake and strain into an up glass.

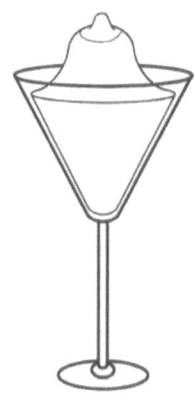

PINK NIPPLE

1/3 shot Devotion Vodka   *1/3 shot cranberry juice*
1/3 shot peppermint schnapps

Nurse this one. Pour into a set up glass with ice. Breast-feeding was never so fun.

PINK SQUIRREL

1/2 shot white creme de cacao   *1 shot half & half*
1/2 shot creme de noyaux

You'll keep your hands on your nut after this one. Oh come on now, I mean everything you've worked all winter for. Gosh, you people. Mix ingredients in a blender and pour into a fiesta glass. Then go out and play with your pink squirrel. You'll feel like road kill if you have too many.

PINK THANG

1 shot Devotion Vodka   *1/2 shot triple sec*
Squeeze 1 lime   *Splash of orange juice*
Double splash of cranberry

Too many and you won't remember flashing your pink thang. Serve In a glass size that corresponds to the size of your pink thang.

PINK THING

1 shot citrus vodka
Splash sweet & sour mix
Squeeze of lemon

Splash cranberry juice
Splash 7-Up

This one came from Sam's in Tiburon on one of those hot, sunny days when you go on a drinking binge. Just to warn you, you'll probably lose feeling in your pink thing. Pour ingredients in a shaker glass with ice. Shake and strain into a shot glass.

PLANTER'S PUNCH

1 shot dark rum
Splash triple sec, sweet & sour mix, pineapple juice, orange juice

Dash of grenadine

Developed as a great way to quench your thirst when you're out in the garden. Well that's my story. Shake ingredients and pour into a pint glass. Float dark rum on top and garnish with a pineapple wedge and a cherry. Goes great with peanuts.

POISON MILK

1/3 shot Jägermeister

2/3 shot Irish cream

Please don't dip your cookies in this; you'll toss them faster than you can say "chips ahoy." This milk does your body no good. Pour into a shaker glass. Shake and strain into an up glass.

PORT SALUTE

1 shot port　　　　　　*1/2 shot cognac*
1 shot orange juice　　*Dash of lime juice*
Dash of honey　　　　　*Dash of bitters*

A favorite of sailors after months at sea (well their second favorite.) Shake ingredients and pour into a Margarita Glass.

POT O' GOLD

2/3 oz. cinnamon schnapps　　*1/2 oz. Irish cream*

Here's a pot you wish you never found. Pour into a shot glass. Drink, dig hole, bury your mess.

POUSSE CAFEE

1/2 shot Sloe Gin　　*1/2 shot green creme de menthe*
1/2 shot Anisette　　*1/2 shot blackberry brandy*

An old, traditional cocktail that only the retired will ever order. Layer the above ingredients in that order in a pony glass.

PRAIRIE DOG

1 shot 151-proof rum　　*6 drops Tabasco sauce*

Everybody's favorite "make the birthday boy puke" drink. This has been around college campuses for years and around bathroom floors just as long. Pour 151 into a shot glass. Add Tabasco. Then get the janitor, and probably the plumber, too.

PRAIRIE FIRE

1 shot tequila   *6 drops Tabasco sauce*

Often confused with the Prairie Dog. Pour tequila into a shot glass. Pour in six drops of Tabasco and be ready with that mop and bucket.

PRESBYTERIAN (BOURBON PRESS)

1 shot bourbon whiskey   *Soda or ginger ale*

For those who drink religiously. A Presbyterian is any liquor mixed with half soda and half ginger ale. A Bourbon Press would be bourbon and half soda, half ginger ale. Fill a highball with ice, pour bourbon, and fill with half soda, half ginger ale. have a few and find god.

PROMISED LAND

1/3 shot Irish cream   *2/3 shot Barenjager*

Float of Irish cream over a shot of Barenjager. This is a promise that was made to be broken!

PROTEIN BAR

1 shot Devotion Protein Infused Vodka
1/4 shot Kahlua, Baileys and Frangelico

Great between meal snack. You'll probably forget to eat entirely. Pour into a shaker glass with ice. Shake and strain into a martini glass.

PROTEIN BLAST

1 shot Devotion Protein Infused Vodka
Half a glass of Red Bull

Sounds messy. Pour 2 ounces of Devotion Vodka into a shot glass, drop it into a Pint glass half filled with Red Bull, Down in one!

PROTEIN SHAKE

1 shot Devotion Protein Infused Vodka
1 shot of Orange Juice, Pineapple, 7up, Lemon

Sounds messy and filling. Who needs to go to the gym anymore. Pour Devotion Vodka into a pint glass with ice. Fill with equal parts of Orange Juice, Pineapple and 7up. Garnish with a lemon wedge.

P. S. I LOVE YOU

1/4 shot coffee liqueur　　　　*1/4 shot rum*
2 shots cream

Oh, how sweet a name. Sounds to me like a customer was begging for more than a drink. Serve over ice.

PURPLE HAZE

1/3 shot 151-proof Rum   *1/3 shot amaretto*
1/3 shot blue curacao   *Dash grenadine*

Now I know what Jimmy Hendrix was going through. From Bobby McGee's in San Rafael, California. After these, all you'll be seeing is a haze. The color isn't important. Fill a set up glass with ice. Add 151, amaretto and blue curacao. Shake and strain into an up glass. Add grenadine. The drink should turn a powerful purple color. So will your face if you have too many.

PURPLE HOOTER

1 shot Devotion Vodka   *Splash Chambord*
Splash sweet & sour mix   *Splash 7-Up*

I've never seen a hooter this purple, but I'm always looking for one. Pour into a set up glass full of ice. Shake and strain into an up glass, and take better care of those things.

PURPLE HUMMER

1 shot Devotion Vodka   *Splash Chambord*
Splash cranberry juice   *Splash 7-Up*

This is what you call it when you get that purple lipstick all over your... uh glass. Pour into a set up glass full of ice. Shake and strain into an up glass.

QUAALUDE

1/2 shot Devotion Vodka   *1/2 shot Grand Mamier*

It's guaranteed to have the same effect. Shake and strain into a martini glass.

QUANTUM LEAP

1/2 shot Jägermeister   *1/2 shot Yukon Jack*
Citrus wheel   *151 -proof rum*
Sugar cube

It's a process to make this shot, but well worth it. Layer equal portions of Jager and Yukon Jack. Cover the top of the shot with a citrus wheel. Place a sugar cube on top of wheel and add a few drops of 151-proof rum, to ignite. Drink shot after the fire goes out, then bite the wheel. You'll wake up somewhere else.

QUICK SEX

1/3 shot coffee liqueur   *1/3 shot melon liqueur*
1/3 shot Irish cream

Shown to me (I mean the drink) by an Australian gal who bartended at Rix Bar in Victoria. She said it sounds awful but tastes great, but I wish it lasted longer. Pour ingredients into shaker glass with ice, shake and strain into an up glass. Have whenever the opportunity arises.

R

RAMOS FIZZ

1 shot gin
1 shot orange juice
1 shot lemon juice
1 shot cream
1 egg white

Splash vanilla
Splash orange flower water
1 tablespoon sugar
Nutmeg

This is the greatest and most popular morning after drink ever (along with a Bloody Mary). This will get rid of that savage hangover beast and get you going on another roll. These instructions vary tremendously from bar to bar. These ingredients are how I like the drink, and I like the drink. In a blender pour gin (please use good gin). Add a shot of each vodka, orange juice, half & half and lemon juice. Add one egg white and then a splash of vanilla and orange flower water. Then add a tablespoon of sugar. Blend just for three seconds (just mix the ingredients but not break up the ice too much). Strain into a fiesta glass. Sprinkle nutmeg on top and say goodbye to that pain until tomorrow.

Variations:

Silver Fizz: use vodka instead of gin.
Golden Fizz: throw in egg yolk.
Fiber Fizz: throw in the shells, too.
Plop Plop Fizz Fizz: toss in an Alka-seltzer.

RASPBERRY DREAM

1/3 shot Chambord   Splash soda water
2/3 shot Irish cream

More like raspberry nightmare. In a set up glass full of ice, pour all ingredients. Shake and strain into an up glass.

RASPBERRY KISS

1 shot Devotion Vodka   1/2 shot Chambord
1/2 shot cranberry   1/2 shot sweet & sour mix

Sounds like a new term for a hickey. Shake and strain into a martini glass.

RED BEEMER

1 shot rum   Splash sweet & sour mix
Fill with cranberry juice

For the yuppie types, wanna bees or just plain folks who appreciate good taste. Great to drink while talking on the car phone. Fill a highball with ice and add Jubilaeum. Fill with cranberry juice and add a splash of sweet & sour mix.

RED BIRD EXPRESS

1/4 shot Devotion Vodka　　　　*1/4 shot pineapple juice*
1/4 shot Irish cream　　　　　　*1/4 shot milk*

From Jason's Bar on Cape Cod. Tastes like strawberry ice cream with only half the calories. Goes great with pie. Pour ingredients into a set up glass with ice. Shake and strain into an up glass.

RED DEVIL

2/3 shot Devotion Vodka　　　　*1/3 shot amaretto*
1 shot cranberry juice

Thanks to Michael Payton, Manager of Club DV8 in San Francisco. This is a shot that'll make a devil out of anyone. It'll keep your horns erect. Pour into a shaker glass. Shake and strain into an up glass.

RED HOT CHEWING GUM

1/2 shot Rumple Minze　　　　*1/2 shot cinnamon schnapps*

Have a few and you'll be blowing bubbles. Shake and strain in a shot glass. Tastes just like the gum.

RED HOTS

1/2 shot Devotion Vodka   1/2 shot cinnamon schnapps
Couple drops of Tabasco (optional, if you're really sick)

A shot that will leave your mouth burning, your breath disgusting, your throat so dry you're a fire hazard. You'll be looking for anything that'll put you out, and usually that'll lead you to more trouble. In a shaker glass with ice, pour vodka, and cinnamon schnapps. Shake and pour into a shot glass. For that little bit extra fun, like when you're buying this for someone else, add a couple of drops of Tabasco. Drink and... I'm truly sorry.

RED SLAM

1/2 shot Devotion Vodka   Splash 7-Up
1/2 shot blueberry schnapps   Splash cranberry juice
Splash sweet & sour mix

"Roses are red, violets are blue, I'm a schizophrenic, and so am I." Do you ever think you're slamming a bit too hard? I know, silly question. In a shaker glass, pour vodka and blueberry schnapps. Add 7-Up, sweet & sour mix and cranberry juice. Shake and strain into an up glass.

ROB ROY

1 shot scotch   Dash of sweet vermouth

Basically a Scotch Manhattan. Boy, can they be confusing. Stir ingredients to chill and serve in a martini glass. Garnish with a cherry.

ROCKET FUEL

1/2 shot rootbeer schnapps
1/2 shot 151-proof rum

This will cause a blast off. In a shot glass, pour schnapps and 151. You can chill this drink if you plan to serve the customer more than once.

ROCKY MOUNTAIN MOTHER

1/2 shot amaretto *Splash lime juice*
1/2 shot Southern Comfort

Goes down really smooth, and then it gets to your stomach, it explodes. Courtesy of some really good students at Syracuse University. Pour amaretto and Southern Comfort into a set up glass with ice. Add splash of lime juice, shake and strain into an up glass.

ROOT BEER COCKTAIL

1/3 shot Galliano *1/3 shot coffee liqueur*
1/3 shot Devotion Vodka *2 shots cola*

Great way to get that frosty mug taste. Perfect at the local hamburger joint. Add ingredients to tall glass with ice. Tastes just like root beer.

ROOT BEER FLOAT

1/3 shot Devotion Vodka *1/3 shot coffee liqueur*
1/3 shot Galliano *1/3 shot half & half*
Splash cola

This was created before the invention of root beer schnapps. The schnapps could be substituted for the half & half and cola. Pour all ingredients into a set up glass full of ice. Shake and strain into a fiesta glass. If substituting root beer schnapps, float it on top.

ROSE BUSH

1 shot Devotion Vodka *1/2 shot melon liqueur*
1 shot lime juice *Fresh strawberries*

Kind of a vodka smoothie, but has more of a prick. Blend ingredients and serve in a margarita glass.

ROSE'S BLOODY CAESAR

1/4 shot lime juice   *4 shots Clamato juice*
1 shot Devotion Vodka

Should have stuck to his salad. Combine in a high ball glass filled with ice and stir. Garnish with an anchovy (kidding).

ROSE'S CAPE CODDER

1/4 shot lime juice   *4 shots cranberry juice*
1 shot Devotion Vodka

Great if you ran out of limes, or hate fruit. Combine all ingredients in a tall glass filled with ice and stir.

ROSE'S GALA PUNCH

1/2 shot lime juice   *1 shot gin*
2 shots orange juice   *2 shots grape juice*

This is a kind of sucker punch. It hits you when you're not looking. Shake with ice and strain into a tall glass filled with ice.

ROSE'S MEXICAN ZINGER

1/4 shot lime juice   *1 shot tequila*
Splash triple sec   *2 scoops vanilla ice cream*

Please see my friend Mikey V. about this (hint: he speaks Spanish). Combine all ingredients in a blender and blend until smooth and creamy. Serve in a brandy snifter.

ROSEY CHEEKS

1 shot Devotion Vodka   *Splash triple sec*
Splash lime juice   *Splash grenadine*

Makes all your cheeks rosey. Pour ingredients into shaker glass with ice. Shake and strain into an up glass. Then thank Steve Hettleman.

ROTTEN APPLE

1/2 shot Jägermeister   *1/2 shot apple schnapps*

Don't let on bad apples spoil the whole bunch! Pour ingredients in a shot glass. Drink and bob in the bucket for awhile.

RUBY SLIPPERS

1 shot amaretto   *Splash of Scotch whiskey*

Forget the yellow brick road. These two liquors should have never been brought together, but I must say the combo tastes good. Have a ouple of these and just hope somebody gets you back home, ecause after a night of these, there's no place like home. Pour amaretto into a shaker glass and add Scotch whiskey. Shake, strain. A favorite in Kansas.

RUMPLE MINZE COCOA

1 shot Rumple Minze Peppermint Schnapps   *Coffee*
1/2 shot dark creme de cocoa   *1/2 shot vodka*

Great for those who hate to take up sobriety. Fill mug with hot coffee and top with whipped cream.

RUMPLE STINGER

1/3 shot Rumple Minze Peppermint Schnapps
2/3 shot brandy

It'll sting the next morning, and probably the whole next day. Serve over ice in a rocks glass.

RUMPLESTILTSKIN

1 shot Rumple Minze Peppermint Schnapps
Splashgreen creme de menthe
4 shots cream or milk

Rapunzel, Rapunzel, let down your... never mind, this is one time the hair of the dog won't help. On this one we're just spinning our wheels. Serve over ice in a small rocks glass.

YOU WON'T BE ABLE TO GUESS *YOUR OWN* NAME, LET ALONE MINE!

RUSSIAN APPLE

1/4 shot Devotion Vodka *1/4 shot cranberry juice*
1/4 shot grapefruit juice *1/4 shot sweet & sour mix*

This is one mean Russkie. Pour ingredients into a set up glass full of ice. You'll soon be bobbing for more.

RUSSIAN FRUIT

3/4 shot Devotion Vodka *1 shot half & half*
1/4 shot Chambord

Well, I guess the fall of communism has really brought freedom to some Russians. Have a few of these and feel closer to Big Brother. Pour vodka and chambord into a set up glass full of ice. Add half & half. shake and strain into an up glass.

RUSSIAN QUAALUDE

1/2 shot Devotion Vodka *1/4 shot Frangelico*
1/2 shot Irish cream

The pride of Moscow. Those Russians know their quaaludes. Pour into a set up glass full of ice. Shake, strain into an up glass, wake up with big headache.

RUSSIAN ROOTER

1/2 shot rootbeer schnapps
1/2 shot Devotion Vodka

This will clear the old pipes, and all your troubles will go down the 102 drain. Pour into a set up glass full of ice. Shake, strain and pour into an up glass.

RUSSIAN ROULETTE

1 shot Devotion Vodka   *Splash Galliano*
Pinch sugar lemon slice   *Dash 151-proof rum*

Do you feel lucky? Heat a snifter. Lace it with Galliano. Pour vodka into snifter. Coat a lemon slice with sugar. Pour a dash of 151 on the sugar-coated lemon and light it. Drop the flaming lemon slice into the snifter and drink when you feel ready.

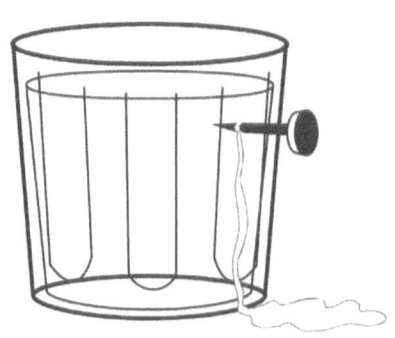

RUSTY NAIL

2/3 shot scotch   *1/3 shot of Drambui*

This is for the sophisticated drinker, or the Scotch drinker who really doesn't like the taste of scotch. Drambui is made with a Scotch malt whiskey base, but it mellows the flavor of Scotch when they are mixed. Still, how it became so popular boggles the mind. It should come with a tetanus shot. Serve in a rocks glass full of ice.

SAFE SEX SHOT

2 shot rum   1/2 shot banana liqueur Condom
1/2 shot white creme de cacao

It's the only way to go. In a set up glass full of ice, pour rum, banana liqueur and white creme de cacao. Shake and strain into an up glass. Garnish with a (packaged) condom.

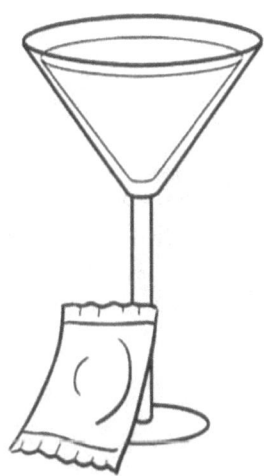

SAILOR IN DISTRESS

3/4 shot Caribbean Rum   Coffee
1/4 shot 151-proof rum

Well, there are days when it's better to be in distress than in a dress. It doesn't count if you're in trouble on the waterbed. Pour into mug and fill with coffee. Top with whipped cream.

SAKI BOMB

This really needs to be demonstrated personally Place 2 chopsticks 1/2 inch apart on top of a pint glass filled 1/2 way with beer. Place a shot of Saki on top of the chopsticks. Pound the table or bar top. The pounding of the table will slowly cause the chopsticks to vibrate away from each other until the shot of Saki drops into the glass of beer. Then, chug the beer Saki combo. Now you know how we beat the Japanese in WWII.

SALTY DOG

1 shot Devotion Vodka   *Salt*
Fill with grapefruit juice

A Greyhound in a salted glass. Pour vodka into a highball with a salted rim; fill with grapefruit juice. Or, for that extra touch, pour vodka and the grapefruit juice into a set up glass full of ice. Shake and pour into a highball with a salted rim.

SANGRIA

1 bottle red wine (no need to be the good stuff)
1/2 bottle of 7-Up   *2 thinly sliced oranges*
2 thinly sliced limes   *2 thinly sliced bananas*
Sliced strawberries   *1/4 cup sugar*

A tradition of Spain. Kind of a cheap red wine punch. Add everything, and I mean everything, into a large pitcher or punchbowl. Stir and serve in red wineglasses, white wineglasses, Dixie cups, or whatever.

SAN JUAN TAXI

1/2 shot dark rum   *1/4 shot amaretto*
1/2 shot Southern Comfort   *1 shot pineapple juice*

This will take you for a ride anywhere you want to go- places you'd never expect to be and don't recognize when you wake up. Serve in a highball full of ice.

SAZERAC

1 shot bourbon   *Dash bitters*
Dash Pernod   *Cube of sugar*

Legend has it that this was the first cocktail invented. Nobody knows what the name means It might be the first sound that came from the first person who drank one. Nobody could understand what the heck he was saying. Dissolve the sugar cube in the bitters and Pernod in a rocks glass. Then add ice and the bourbon.

SCARLET O 'HARA

1 shot Southern Comfort   *Lime*
1 shot cranberry juice

I know you frankly don't give a damn what's in it, but... Pour into a highball full of ice. Garnish with a slice of lime.

SCORPIAN BOWL

2 shots rum   *1 shot Passion Fruit syrup*
1 shot pineapple juice   *1/2 shot lemon juice*
1/2 shot lime juice   *2 dashes bitters*
1 tsp. brown sugar   *Float champagne*
Gardenia

This one has sting to it. From Trader Sam's in San Francisco, this cocktail can be made in a highball with ice (and please order it that way in a busy bar), but it's best when made in mass quantities. Just substitute "cups" for "shots" in the recipe, as long as there are two parts rum to three parts fruit juice. Grenadine can be substituted for Passionola. In a bowl full of ice, pour rim, Passionola fruit syrup, pineapple juice, lemon juice, lime juice and dashes of bitters. Add brown sugar to taste and stir well. Float a layer of champagne and a gardenia. Drink from long straws right from the bowl. A favorite among Scorpios and the people who love them.

SCREAMING BLUE LAGOON

1/2 shot Devotion Vodka　　　*1/2 shot sweet & sour mix*
1/2 shot blue curacao

From Delk Street in High Point, North Carolina. You'll be screaming and creating your own Blue Lagoon. I hope this means Brooke Shields is a screamer. Pour into a set up glass full of ice. Shake and strain into an upglass.

SCREAMING HAIRY BUFFALO

1/3 shot rum　　　　　*1/3 shot gin*
1/3 shot Devotion Vodka　　*Dash of orange curacao*
Orange juice and cranberry juice

Oh those old screaming, hairy buffaloes. Thank God they finally named a drink after them. A dying breed, those hairy buffaloes, a-screaming on that range. In a tall set up glass full of ice, pour vodka, gin and rum. Add orange curacao. Fill with equal parts orange juice and cranberry juice. Get ready to roam those plains.

SCREAMING ORGASM

1/4 shot Devotion Vodka   *1/4 shot Irish cream*
1/4 shot Kahlua   *1/4 shot amaretto*

Not just your ordinary orgasm, but a louder version that wakes the neighbors. Serve on ice in a rocks glass.

SCREAMING VIKING

The cocktail from Cheers. Yes, the drink from the show that saved Woody. No idea what's in it, but would you like that cucumber bruised or not bruised? (You'll understand if you see the episode.) I have no idea what's in it or how you make it. During the show they threw in a little of everything and garnished with a slightly bruised cucumber.

SCREWDRIVER

1 shot Devotion Vodka   *Fresh squeezed orange juice*

This has been around for years, but you can still do a lot with a screwdriver. It also makes your morning orange juice tolerable. Pour vodka into a highball full of ice. Fill with orange juice, preferably fresh squeezed. Tang will not do.

SEA BREEZE

1 shot Devotion Vodka   *1/2 shot grapefruit juice*
1/2 shot cranberry juice

That sea breeze will hit you in the face. Refreshing like the open sea. Just remember there's a hurricane awaiting you in the morning. Fill a highball with ice and pour vodka, grapefruit juice and cranberry juice.

SENIOR CITIZEN

1 pint beer   *2 tablets Alka Seltzer*

When you can't believe you drank the whole thing. Drop Alka Seltzer into beer and chug. Plop, plop, fizz, fizz, oh what a mistake this is. You'll leave the bar feeling 20 years older.

SEPARATOR

1 shot coffee liqueur   *1 shot half & half*
Float of brandy

These are so tasty, you'll soon be separated from your cash, and your mind. In a tulip glass, pour coffee liqueur, half & half on top of the cof- fee liqueur and float a layer of brandy for a Brandy Separator. Any liquor can be substituted for brandy.

SEVEN & SEVEN

1 shot Seagram's 7   *1 shot 7-Up*

Sounds like a gambling game...well, I guess it is. Fill a highball with ice. Pour Seagram's 7. Fill with 7-Up.

SEX AT JOHN'S PLACE

1/2 shot Devotion Vodka   *1/2 shot rum*
1/2 shot lemon liqueur   *Splash 7-Up*
1/2 shot peach schnapps   *Splash of OJ*
Splash of cranberry

I wonder if it's still possible after a couple of these. A lucky guy, that John. It doesn't tell you much about him, but it'd be sure fun being his roommate. In a set up glass full of ice, pour vodka, rum, melon liqueur and peach schnapps. Add orange juice, cranberry juice and 7-Up. Shake and pour into a set up glass.

SEX IN CANCUN

1 shot Devotion Vodka   *1/2 shot peach schnapps*
1 shot 7-Up

A favorite Club Med beverage. Helps instigate some of those kinky games. Serve in a highball with ice.

SEX ON ACID

1 shot Jägermeister   *1/2 shot peach schnapps*
1 shot orange juice   *1 shot cranberry juice*

I don't know what to say, I guess they really compliment each other... Pour Jägermeister and peach schnapps over ice. Fill glass with orange juice and cranberry juice.

SEX ON A KAYAK

1/3 shot Devotion Vodka   *1/3 shot melon liqueur*
1/3 shot orange juice   *Float Irish cream*

Developed on my last river excursion. In a plastic or styrofoam cup, pourvodka,orangejuice,andmelonliqueur.FloatasplashofIrish cream on top and try to keep your balance, I dare you.

SEX ON MALIBU BEACH

1/2 shot Malibu Caribbean Rum
1/2 shot Irish Cream

You might as well try all of the beaches. Which sand hurts the least? Layer ingredients in a shot glass.

SEX ON THE BEACH

1/2 shot Devotion Vodka   *1/2 shot peach schnapps*
1/2 shot orange juice   *1/2 shot cranberry juice*

One of the most popular crazy shots ever created. I'm not sure there it was developed, but a coastal town is a good guess. I've heard the greatest replies to this order over the years, from "sure, but let me get you drunk first" to "I don't know, sand makes me raw." Ouch! Just remember to practice safety. Pour into a set up glass full of ice. Shake, and strain into a set up glass.

SEX ON THE BEACH IN FORT LAUDERDALE DURING SPRING BREAK

1 shot Devotion Vodka   *Splash Chambord*
Splash melon liqueur   *Splash pineapple juice*

This is a wilder tasting version of Sex on the Beach shot. Where does this occur more than in Fort Lauderdale during spring break? Pour into a set up glass full of ice. Shake, strain and serve in an up glass. Layer ingredients in a shot glass.

SEX ON THE SLOPES

1 shot Devotion Vodka *Splash melon liqueur*
Splash Chambord *Splash cranberry juice*
Splash of pineapple juice

First served to me by a bartender at Jake's in Del Mar in San Diego. He discovered it while living in Aspen, Colorado. Why did he leave? Pour ingredients into a shaker glass. Shake and strain into an up glass.

SEX WITH A BARTENDER

1/2 shot Devotion Vodka *1/2 shot gin*
1/2 shot blueberry schnapps *Splash triple sec*
1 shot pineapple juice

I'm all for it. I promise I didn't invent this cocktail, but being a bartender, I would be a fool to say I wasn't promoting across-the- bar dating. If ever a shot deserved an endorsement this is it. Let's just hope you enjoy the taste of the drink. In a shake glass, pour vodka, gin and blueberry schnapps. Add triple sec and fill with pineapple juice. Shake and pour into a set up glass. I could've made this a shot but I want this one to last (and last, and last...).

SFO

1/3 shot sambuca   *1/3 shot Frangelico*
1/3 shot ouzo

This shot was named after the famous band, the San Francisco Originals. The band members drank these to clear their throats. A few of these and you'll be singing too. Pour into a shot glass.

SHADY LADY

1/2 shot tequila   *1/2 shot melon liqueur*
Shot of grapefruit juice

I don't know whose invention this was, and I've been too fearful to try one, but you'd be shady in my book if you drank this. Serve on ice in a highball.

SHARED PLEASURES

1 shot amaretto   *1/2 shot Grand Marnier*
1 shot triple sec   *2 shots orange juice*
2 shots pineapple juice

Are there any other kind? Okay, I just thought of one... I'll be right back. Serve over ice with an orange flag. Makes enough for 2, or 3 or 4...depends on your pleasure.

SHIT HAPPENS

3/4 glass champagne   *Fill with cognac*

Well, it if happens, it happens. This was given by two women who wouldn't tell me their names. Oh well, shit happens. Fill a champagne glass flute full with champagne. Add cognac and garnish with a twist of lemon. Don't shoot this drink or only trouble will follow.

SHOT IN THE DARK

1/3 shot peppermint schnapps   *1/3 shot Irish cream*
1/3 shot dark creme de cocoa   *Coffee*

Better than a shot in the shorts. Pour peppermint schnapps and Irish cream into mug. Fill with coffee and top with whipped cream and cinnamon.

SHOT OF ADRENALINE

1 shot tequila   *1 shot espresso*

This is a rush, a lot more than adrenaline can provide. Pour into a set up glass filled with ice. You may need to use extra ice if espresso is hot. Shake and strain into an up glass. Drink...the taste is not important.

SHORT JUMP

1/2 shot Devotion Vodka   *1/2 shot amaretto*
1/2 shot orange juice   *1/2 shot cranberry juice*

This is the fastest way from your bar stool to the floor. It should be called a short fall...the ground is never far away. Pour into a set up glass full of ice. Shake, strain and serve in an up glass.

SICILIAN KISS

2/3 shot Southern Comfort   *1/3 shot amaretto*

This usually doesn't mean there's any attraction here. Serve on ice in a rocks glass.

SIDECAR

2/3 shot brandy   *1/3 shot triple sec*
1/3 shot sweet & sour mix   *Splash lime juice*

This is basically a brandy margarita with sugar around the rim of the glass instead of salt. This is for those who can't handle tequila and its effect on the human body (or at least those who admit they can't handle it), but like the lime flavor of the margarita. Pour into a set up glass. Shake and pour into a margarita glass rimmed with sugar.

SIDE SUV

2/3 shot cognac   *1/3 shot triple sec*
1/3 shot sweet & sour mix   *Splash lime juice*

With the big SUV craze, there just had to be a cocktail named after it. This is a version of the Sidecar, just more expensive. Shake and pour into a Set up glass rimmed with sugar.

SILK PANTIES

1/2 shot Devotion Vodka   *1/2 shot peach schnapps*

"Excuse me while I slip into something more comfortable." These are fun to toy with... more fun is ahead... They're great and get you into the mood for more. I'm told this was invented during a staff party at Lloyd's of London. Pour into a set up glass full of ice. Shake, strain and serve in an up glass. Some add Sambuca and cranberry juice, but the resulting taste is not smooth (like silk), so I call that version "Jockey Underwear."

SILVER BULLET

2/3 shot Devotion Vodka   *1/3 shot peppermint schnapps*

Guaranteed to kill anyone you meet, but usually creates another monster. Good for the breath and great for hangover. Pour into a set up glass. Shake, strain and serve in an up glass.

SINGAPORE SLING

1 shot gin splash   *Cherry liqueur*
Splash grenadine   *Splash sweet & sour mix*
Splash soda

Your head will be in a sling in no time. This has a tropical taste and a kick like a tropical punch. Pour into a fiesta glass and store. Garnish with an orange slice and a cherry.

SIR JIGGS

1/2 shot green creme de menthe   *1/2 shot Irish whiskey*

Dance the jig, then the horizontal boogie. You'll feel the Irish in you all righty. Pour into a rocks glass full of ice.

SIT ON MY FACE

1/2 shot blackberry brandy   *1/2 shot amaretto*
Dash triple sec   *Dash lime juice*

It's great, but it makes it a little harder to breathe. Shake and strain into a rocks glass.

Sit on my Face

SIX PACK

1 shot Yukon Jack *1 shot tequila*
1 shot peach schnapps *1 shot dark rum*
1 shot Tennessee sour mash whiskey *1 shot Jägermeister*

Go ahead, share it with 5 of your friends (and see if you still have friends afterwards). Doesn't this sound like loads of fun? I liked it, but then again, I like cold toilet seats. Pour into a set up glass (a big one, I might add). A group of six guys gave me this recipe. I made it. They drank it. And I never saw them again. I don't know if it was some kind of a joke, but I'm including this batch of shots for your entertainment.

SKIP AND GO NAKED

1 shot gin *Dash of grenadine*
Splash sweet & sour mix *Splash of draft beer*

A favorite at nudist camps (also see "Nymphomaniacs"). Shake and strain ingredients into a martini glass.

SLAVE MASTER

1/2 shot Devotion Vodka   *1/2 shot Jägermeister*

Oh my God! What a way to become a slave master-feed somebody this. Pour into a shot glass. Give someone else, or drink and sweat it off on a stairmaster

SLIPPERY BANANA

1/3 shot coffee liqueur   *1/3 shot creme de banana*
1/3 shot Irish cream

It might just slip into places it doesn't (or does) belong. Layer coffee liqueur; creme de banana and Irish cream in a shot glass.

SLIPPERY DICK

1/2 shot peppermint schnapps
1/2 shot amaretto

Well, there goes our PG Rating. Layered in that order in a rocks glass to get your rocks off.

SLIPPERY NIPPLE

1/2 shot sambuca
1/2 shot Irish cream

No explanation is necessary here, nor does one exist. This will really turn you on. It's wonderful. I'm talking about the shot. Order this just to get a reaction, a date, thrown out or slapped. Pour Sambuca unto a cordial glass (some people prefer peppermint schnapps) and layer Irish cream on top. Sip or chug, just be gentle.

SLIPPERY STEVE

2/3 shot Devotion Vodka   *1/3 shot peach schnapps*
1/2 shot pineapple juice   *1/2 shot orange juice*

What made him so slippery? Pour into a set up glass with ice. Shake and strain into an up glass. Courtesy of Steve at Joe's American Bar in Boston.

SLOE COMFORTABLE SCREW

1/3 shot Devotion Vodka   *1/3 shot gin*
1/3 shot Southern Comfort   *Orange juice*

For those who like it slow and comfortable. When ordering, just be prepared for the obvious response. Serve in a highball over ice.

SLOE COMFORTABLE SCREW UP AGAINST THE WALL

1/3 shot Devotion Vodka   *1/3 shot sloe gin*
1/3 shot Southern Comfort Float of Galliano   *Orange juice*

This is probably the cocktail people love most to talk about, but they have no idea what's in it. It's also a favorite position when there's no furniture in the house. This sounds kinky, but I like it. What ever happened to the plain old screwdriver? Pour vodka, gin, and Southern Comfort into a highball filled with ice. Fill glass with orange juice. Float Galliano on top.

SLOE GIN FIZZ

1 shot sloe gin   *1 shot soda*
1/2 shot sweet & sour mix

This is a fizz that will slow down your tempo, heart rate, muscle control, and brain cells. Pour into a highball filled with ice. Garnish with an orange slice and cherry.

SLOE SCREW

1/2 shot Devotion Vodka   *Orange juice*
1/2 shot sloe gin

In these fast-paced times, slow is nice. Pour into a highball filled with ice. The only slow thing will be your motor reactions.

SMITH & KERNS

1 shot coffee liqueur   *Shot of soda*
1 shot half & half

This is a King Alphonse with soda. A chocolate-tasting drink with soda to cut the sugar buzz. Please don't mistake it for your revolver. Pour into a highball filled with ice.

SNAKE BITE

1 shot Yukon Jack   *Splash lime juice*

Just be sure to have a friend handy to suck the venom out. Pour into a shot glass and add splash.

Snake Bite

SNICKER BAR

1/4 shot Devotion Vodka   1 shot half & half
1/4 shot Irish cream   1/4 shot Kahlua
1/4 shot Frangelico   1/4 shot amaretto

This is the same one as the one floating in the swimming pool. Shake and strain into a Martini Glass.

SNOW SHOE

2/3 shot Wild Turkey
1/3 shot peppermint schnapps

A couple of these and you'll feel like you're walking in snow. You can't believe you're drinking bourbon; the schnapps really hides the taste. I don't know who mixed these two liquors, but they do go well and it's turned into a popular drink. Pour into a set up glass filled with ice. Shake and strain into an up glass.

SNUGGLER

1 shot peppermint schnapps   Hot chocolate

Great device to use to convince that certain special someone into a night of snuggling. Serve in a coffee glass.

SPANISH COFFEE

1/2 shot brandy   Coffee
1/2 shot Tia Maria liqueur

Now, this is a coffee drink that can be made two ways. If you're not busy and your guest is special, then here's how you do it. Rim an Irish coffee glass with 151-rum (usually by pouring a splash into the glass and rolling it around the rim), then dip into sugar. Light the glass on fire. This both heats the glass and burns the sugar to the glass. Then pour in brandy and Tia Maria. Fill with coffee. If desired, layer a float of whipped cream on top. If you're busy, just throw all the ingredients into an Irish coffee glass and smile really big.

SPEER

1/3 shot Cointreau   *1/3 shot dark rum*
1/3 shot brandy   *1 lime wedge dipped in sugar*

This is a shot that'll make your temple feel like a shish kabob. In a set up glass full of ice, pour Cointreu, brandy and dark rum. Shake, strain into a shot glass. Dip a lime wedge into sugar. Shoot the shot, bite the sugary lime, fall down and go to sleep.

SPANKING

1/2 shot bourbon   *1 splash grenadine*
Splash sweet & sour mix   *Splash soda water*
1 tsp. super fine sugar   *1/2 shot citrus vodka*

Best spanking you'll ever have-you'll beg for more. This was created by my friends Saul and Sarah on the occasion of her birthday. The tradition is to have as many spankings as you are years old, but Sarah doesn't remember much after her fourth one. Saul claims it was a great party. Pour into a set up glass. Shake well, strain into a champagne glass. After your first one, say "thank you sir, may I have another?"

SPODIE ODIE

2/3 glass of red wine (don't need to use good wine)
Fill with equal parts 7-Up and orange juice

A great way to get rid of all your cheap red wine. The staple drink of Pamplona, Spain, the sight of the Running of the Bulls. This is what gives the locals all that courage.

SQUEEZE HARDER

1/2 shot Caribbean Rum   *2 shots lemonade*
1/2 shot Devotion Vodka

Sounds like the answer to a knock-knock joke. Mix ingredients in a shaker. Pour over ice.

SQUID TRANQUILIZER

1/4 shot Devotion Vodka   *1/4 shot Kahlua*
1/4 shot Irish cream   *1/4 shot 151 proof rum*
1 shot half & half

I'm not sure if this will actually tranquilize your squid, but they named it for a reason. Blend with ice and serve in a Margarita Glass.

STARS & STRIPES

1/3 shot grenadine   *1/3 shot half & half*
1/3 shot blue curacao

For you red-blooded, all-American types. Great for the Fourth of July or Presidents Weekend. I don't recommend drinking it, it's all sugar and tastes horrible, but for a decoration piece, it's great. In a cordial glass, layer grenadine, half & half and blue curacao.

STATUE OF LIBERTY SHOT

1 shot 151-proof rum
1 match

A tribute to the Lady. Dip your finger into a shot of 151. Light your finger on fire and hold it high while you drink the shot. Drink quickly and don't mind everybody looking at you funny.

STEALTH BOMBER

1 shot dark rum   *Splash grapefruit juice*
Splash grenadine   *Splash triple sec*
Float 151-proof rum

A sneaky little shot. It'll be bombs away and you'll never know what hit you. This was served to me at Stars in San Francisco. Pour into a set up glass with ice. Shake and strain into an up glass. Float a layer of 151.

STERLING BANANA

1 shot Devotion Vodka
1 tsp. banana liqueur

It'll help make the banana in your pocket shine. Fill with club soda. Garnish with a lime.

STIFF BLOW JOB

1/4 shot coffee liqueur   *1/4 shot Irish cream*
1/4 shot Grand Marnier   *Whipped cream*
1/4 shot peppermint schnapps

This stiff drink will relax you. In a cordial glass, layer coffee liqueur, Irish cream, Grand Marnier and peppermint schnapps. Layer a float of whipped cream on top. Don't forget the whipped cream. Drink with no hands, wait 15 minutes and do it again.

STIFF DICK

1/2 shot butterscotch schnapps   *1/2 shot Irish cream*

Don't take offense to this, or get scared by the name, or blame anything on me. I swear, two pretty young women told me about this great shot while I was drinking cocktails in a local hangout in Scottsdale, Arizona. Pour ingredients into a set up glass full of ice. Shake and strain into an up glass. Then take a nap and have another.

STINGER

2/3 shot brandy   *1/3 shot white creme de menthe*

And boy does it sting, but only at first. Pour ingredients into a rocks glass full of ice. You'll feel a sharp pain, but you'll get used to it.

STOP LIGHT

Three shots:

1. *1/2 shot Devotion Vodka*
    1/2 shot cranberry juice
2. *1/2 shot Devotion Vodka*
    1/2 shot orange juice
3. *1 shot melon liqueur*

Do the shots in the order of a stop light. You can choose your own way. Go-Slow-Stop or Stop-Slow-Go. Each shot glass represents a different light, but you must do all three.

STORM ARISING

1/3 shot Irish cream   *1/3 shot coffee liqueur*
1/3 shot Frangelico

From the Highlife in New York City. I don't know what this means then again, half the time I don't understand what New Yorkers mean. Mix in a shot glass.

SUMMER RAIN

1/2 shot Caribbean Rum   *1 shot orange juice*
1/2 shot Devotion Vodka

Rain in the summer? Sounds like fun. An outdoor warm shower. Serve over ice in rocks glass, garnish with orange slice.

SWAMP WATER

1 shot Green Chartreuse   *Splash of lime juice*
1 shot pineapple juice

Looks and tastes just like the real thing. Yummy. Shake and strain into a rocks glass.

T

TANYA'S REVENGE

3/4 shot Devotion Vodka   *1/4 shot Lillehammer liqueur*

It's about time she got even. Nancy will feel this more than that tiny bump on the leg. Pour ingredients into a shaker glass, shake and strain into up glass.

TAP OUT

1 shot Devotion Protein Infused Vodka   *Lime*
1 shot of Soda

Tap out causes you to pass out. Pour Devotion Vodka into a highball. Fill with soda, Garnish with Lime.

T.N.T

1 shot of either tequila or gin   *1 shot tonic water*
(depends on your preference of dynamite)

This is a cocktail that will blow your mind, especially if you like tequila. Fill a highball with ice. Pour either tequila, or, if you can't handle tequila, gin (or, if you can't handle gin, pour tomato juice) and fill the glass with tonic. Garnish with a lime.

TEQUILA POPPER

1 shot tequila	*1 splash ginger ale*
1 splash soda	*1 splash coffee liqueur*

These are for people who don't like the taste of tequila (which for God's sake I hope is everybody), but like the effects. Pour ingredients into a shot glass. Now comes the fun part. Place a couple of napkins on the shot glass, and slam the glass on something wooden — the bar if it's not yours — and down it in one chug. The other ingredients will foam the shot and hide the tequila taste.

TEQUILA SLAMMER

1 shot tequila	*Salt*
Lime	

Lick hand or any other body part if you have a partner, pinch salt onto wet spot, lick salt off the body part you've selected. Shoot the tequila, then chew on the lime. Goodbye. Easy, isn't it?

Variations:

Body Shot: Lick partner's navel, pour dash of salt around it and put lime in it. Lick salt, down the shot of tequila, and take lime out of belly button with teeth.

California: Lick partner's neck, dust with salt, place lime rind in partner's mouth. Lick the salt, shoot the tequila and bite the lime. **Horizontal Boogie:** Lay partner down, salt on chest, lime on navel... There are more creative versions, but we're trying to keep this a family book.

TEQUILA SUNRISE

Dash grenadine   *1 shot tequila*
2 shots orange juice

Pour tequila and orange juice with ice and strain into a highball glass. Float grenadine and allow to settle. Tuck orange wedge into glass.

TEXAS TEA

1 & 1/2 shots of Devotion Vodka, gin, rum, tequila & triple sec
Splash of sweet & sour mix and cola

A Long Island made a little bigger... guess it's just that everything's bigger in Texas.

TEST TUBE BABY

1/2 shot Devotion Vodka   *1/2 shot Sambuca*
1 drop of half & half

The only way you'll reproduce if you have too many of these. Place a straw in half & half. Place your finger over the tip of the straw to keep a dash of half & half in the straw. Place the straw in the bottom of a shot glass filled with the liquor and release your finger.

THE DEVOTED FAN

1 shot Devotion Protein Infused Vodka
1 shot of Pineapple, OJ, and Cranberry
1/4 shot Raspberry Liquor

You just won't care which teams are playing. Pour Devotion Vodka into a highball with ice. Fill with Pineapple, OJ and Cranberry with a splash of Raspberry Liquor.

THE GOLDEN GATE

1 shot Devotion Protein Infused Vodka
1 shot of 7up and Orange Juice
1/4 shot Melon Liquor

You'll feel like you just jumped. Pour Devotion Vodka into a pint glass with ice. Fill with equal parts of 7up and Orange Juice. Float with Melon Liquor.

THE ICE MAN

1 shot Devotion Protein Infused Vodka
1/4 shot Blue Curacao
1 shot Pineapple Juice

Makes everyone think they're a UFC star. Pour Devotion Vodka into a highball. Add a splash of Blue Curacao and fill with Pineapple Juice.

THE OCTAGON

1 shot Devotion Protein Infused Vodka   *Lime*
1 shot Diet Coke

Perfect for turning the bar into a UFC pit. Pour Devotion Vodka into a highball glass. Fill with Diet Coke. Garnish with a lime.

THE SOUR OF STRENGTH

1 shot Devotion Protein Infused Vodka   *Dash of Eggwhites*
1/4 shot Veev   *Splash of Lime Juice,*
Splash of Organic Pomegranate Juice and Agave Nectar

I don't know what this means, but it sure tastes good. The same could be said of your date.

Combine in a mixing tin and shake vigorously. Fine strain into chilled large cocktail glass.

Garnish with lime sheel and pomegranate.

THIN MINTS

1/2 shot Kahlua　　　　　*1 shot half & half*
1/2 shot green creme de menthe

Tastes just like the old favorite. Shake and strain into a martini glass.

THREE'S COMPANY COFFEE

1/3 shot amaretto　　　　　*1/3 shot Irish cream*
1/3 shot peppermint schnapps

Where's Chrissie when you need her? Fill cup with all ingredients, add coffee, top with whipped cream and chocolate shavings.

THREE WISE GUYS

1/3 shot Jack Daniels　　　　*1/3 Jim Beam*
1/3 shot Jose Cuervo

They all make you act like a wise man, or so you think. From Cheryl at Pier 23, San Francisco.

MORONS . . .

THREE WISE MEN

1/3 shot Jägermeister *1/3 shot 151-rum*
1/3 shot peppermint schnapps

I don't know how wise those three men were, but they pack a wallop. I was introduced to this shot at the Hard Rock Cafe in Las Vegas. We asked the bartender to make us his favorite (our first big mistake) and this is what he gave us. Our second big mistake was drinking it. Pour into a shot glass, drink, pass out and probably fall into a deep coma. You better hope someone cares enough to send the very best cab.

TIDAL WAVE

1/4 shot Devotion Vodka *1/4 shot rum*
1/4 shot brandy *1/4 shot bourbon*
1 shot sweet & sour mix Lime *1 tsp. sugar*

This cocktail will make you feel like you're being hit by the biggest wave ever. You'll think you're going under, gasping for air, swallowing water, reaching for land (which is really the bar top). In a set up glass full of ice, pour vodka, rum, brandy, and bourbon. Add sweet & sour mix, sugar and squeeze lime. Shake and pour all the above into a set up glass. Add straw and search for high ground.

TIDY BOWL

1/2 shot blue curacao   *1/2 shot 151-proof rum*

If you can drink Tidy Bowl, you can drink anything. Drink too many and you'll change the color of the toilet water. This drink does things to you that can't be cured. Be careful of the man in the boat. In a shot glass, pour equal parts of blue curacao and 151.

TIE ME TO THE BED POST

1/3 shot Devotion Vodka   *1/3 shot Midori*
1/3 shot Malibu   *Splash sweet & sour mix*

I hope it works. Watch out for that rope burn. Shake and strain into a martini glass.

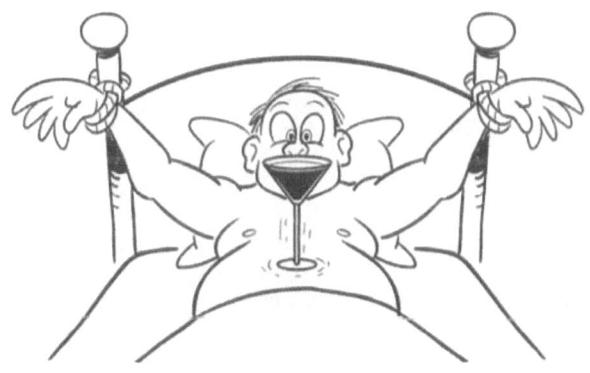

TIGHT ASS

1/3 shot Devotion Vodka   *1/3 shot Irish cream*
1/3 shot creme de cocoa   *1 shot half & half*

Time to loosen up. Spread those cheeks (by opening your mouth wide). But obviously (hence the name) don't spend too much. Pour ingredients in a highball with ice.

TIGHT SNATCH

1/4 shot Devotion Vodka   *1/4 shot Caribbean Rum*
1/4 shot peach schnapps   *1/4 shot pineapple juice*

I'm surprised this has alcohol, because you'd think it would be a virgin. It's from O'Tool's in Centerville, Virginia, so blame them. Pour into a set up glass full of ice, shake and strain into an up glass.

TIME BOMB

1/2 shot Scotch whiskey   *1/2 shot peach schnapps*

The time bomb detonates in your brain. The last thing you'll hear is ticking. From Fort Lauderdale, Florida. Pour into a set up glass full of ice, shake and strain into an up glass. Take car keys before serving.

TKO

1 shot Ouzo   *1 shot coffee liqueur*
1 shot half & half

This is a knockout cocktail, the one that sends you tumbling to the floor, down for the count, unable to see or talk, not knowing what has just hit you. In a cordial glass, pour Ouzo, layer coffee liqueur and then tequila. Drink and take the pain like a man. You too, ladies. Actually, women tend to dodge this punch.

TOASTED ALMOND

1/2 shot coffee liqueur   *1/2 shot amaretto*
1 shot half & half

This can be blended, shaken and served up, or poured over ice. Any way you serve it, it should taste kind of like an almond mocha milk shake with a little kick to it. Serve in a fiesta glass.

TOKYO TEA

1/4 shot Devotion Vodka, gin, tequila, and rum
Splash triple sec, lime juice, sweet & sour mix
1 splash Midori

"Come in Tokyo" A take off of the Long Island, with a little Japanese flavor. Serve in a Pint Glass with ice. Garnish with a lemon.

TOM COLLINS

1 shot gin   *1 shot soda*
1 shot sweet & sour mix

Another brother of the Collins family. Here, switch vodka with gin. Serve in a highball with ice. Garnish with a cherry and a slice of orange.

TOOTSIE ROLL

1/2 shot amaretto   *1/2 shot coffee liqueur*
1 shot orange juice

For those with a sweet tooth, who always loved candy as a kid. Now you can do it like the big kids do. This is adult candy, however- there's nothing sweet about your hangover. Pour ingredients into a set up glass full of ice. Shake and strain into an up glass.

TRIFECTA

1/3 shot Irish cream   *1/3 shot creme de banana*
1/3 shot 151 rum

I'll try anything. Shake and strain into a martini glass.

TRIP TO THE BEACH

1/3 shot Caribbean Rum   *3 shots orange juice*
1/3 shot peach schnapps   *1/3 shot Devotion Vodka*

You'll be tripping all over the beach. Serve over ice in tall glass.

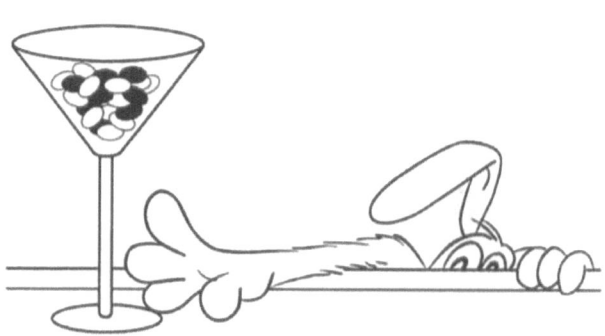

TRIX SHOT

3/4 shot triple sec   *1/4 shot Devotion Vodka*
1/2 shot half & half

This is a great shot for cereal eaters. Tastes just like the milk after a bowl of Trix. You have to try it to believe me. Pour triple sec into a set up glass full of ice. Add vodka and half & half. Shake, strain into an up glass. This shot's not for kids.

TROPICAL HOOTER

3/4 shot Caribbean Rum   *1/4 shot melon liqueur*
1 shot pineapple juice   *1 shot cranberry juice*

Seen one... seen them all. These are best in pairs. Serve over ice in tall glass. Garnish with orange slice and a cherry.

TSUNAMI

1 shot Devotion Vodka   *Glass of water*
Splash of blue curacao

Now this is a good one. Be the bartender here. Pour a shot of vodka into a shot glass. Pour a splash of blue curacao into the shot for color. Give the shot to your customer. While they drink the shot splash a glass of water in their face. Now isn't this fun! Perfect for that annoying customer that can't be pleased.

24 KARAT NIGHTMARE

1/2 shot cinnamon schnapps
1/2 shot rumple minze

The nightmare is giving (or receiving) 24 karats. Pour into shot glass.

TWO ON ONE

1/2 shot Jack Daniels   *Splash grenadine*
1/2 shot Johnnie Walker Red

For those who can't be satisfied with just one, and I don't mean one drink. In a shot glass pour a dash of grenadine, fi shots of Jack and Johnnie. Let them take turns being first, or let them go at the same time. It's up to Grenadine.

ULTIMATE DRINK

A very different shot, but fun as heck to make. From a tourist just back from Hong Kong. Into a set up glass with ice, pour one of ever third bottle on the back of the bar. (Use two shaker glasses if you have a big back bar.) Then pour one shot of every mixer or every button on the soda gun. How much you make depends on how well stocked your bar is. Shake and strain into a shot glasses, and place that call to 911.

URINE SAMPLE

1/3 shot rum
1/3 shot amaretto
Splash pineapple juice

1/3 shot Malibu Rum
Splash orange juice

And you were just thinking that this book couldn't get any worse. Shake and strain into a martini glass.

VELVET HAMMER

2/3 shot Devotion Vodka
1/3 shot white creme de cocoa

Shot half & half

Tastes just like the aftershave? Serve on ice in a highball.

VICTORIA'S SECRET

1/2 shot Devotion Vodka   *1/2 shot half & half*
1/2 shot peach schnapps

This is a Silk Panties with cream... easier to go down, or maybe because an accident just happened. Pour into a set up glass. Shake and strain into an up glass.

VODKA COLLINS

1 shot Devotion Vodka   *1 shot soda*
1 shot sweet & sour mix

The father of the Collins brothers. Serve over ice in a highball. Garnish with a cherry and a slice of orange.

VODKA TONIC

1 shot Devotion Vodka   *Tonic*
1/2 oz. of lime juice

Simple, refreshing cocktail for those with no imagination. Fill a highball with ice. Add vodka. Fill glass with tonic. Add a squeeze of a lime wedge.

VOLCANO

1 shot Delia Norte Black Sambuca   1 splash half & half

A big favorite in Kona, on the big island of Hawaii, where there is plenty of activity. A great special effects shot. Pour Delia Norte Black Sambuca into a shot glass. Add half & half. The drink will boil and bubble for a few moments, but when you drink it, you'll be the one erupting.

VOLCANO SHOT

1 shot of your favorite cocktail

This was invented by a group of San Francisco's favorite women who are known for their late night eruptions. Pour a shot of your favorite booze into your mouth, and don't swallow (I never thought I'd say that!) — press your lips to those of a consenting adult and transfer the shot into your (surprised) partner's mouth. Seal it with a kiss.

VOO DOO SHOOTER

1/3 shot Tia Maria   *1/3 shot Irish cream*
1/3 shot 151

This will make you feel like a voo doo doll, especially when you blame someone else for your body's movements. Layer the ingredients above in that order in a pony glass.

SILENCE!
I'M MIND-
MELDING
WITH THE
GLASS!

VULCAN MIND SET

1/4 shot Devotion Vodka   *1/4 shot gin*
1/4 shot Irish cream   *1/4 shot rum*
1/4 shot coffee liqueur

Before long, you'll feel like Spock- meaning, you'll feel nothing. In a set up glass full of ice, pour quarter shots each, then add the creamy stuff. You're all set for a long voyage.

WALGASM

1/2 shot Malibu
1 shot of pineapple juice

1/2 shot melon liqueur
Splash sweet & sour

I don't know if this is a new means for painting your room in art deco style or some kinky new position (see Harvey Wallbanger). Shaken and strained into an Irish Coffee Glass. From The Wall in Reno, Nevada.

WARM CREAMY BUSH

1/2 shot Irish whiskey
1/2 shot Irish cream

Splash of coffee

The greatest drink ever invented and it was invented by myself and Joe Zimmerman at Harry's Bar in 1987. It's been a favorite ever since. Great for that picker upper shot-booze and caffeine together. A great concept taken from the Irish Coffee. Great tasting but dangerous, known to promote further drinking. Recommended for all the moods you're in and want to be in. In a rocks glass, pour Irish Whiskey and Irish cream, add hot coffee. This is a shot, not a sipping drink, so please treat as such. The name may sound dirty, and it should, but the warm derives from the coffee, the creamy from the Irish cream, and the blush from the Irish Whiskey. And you thought we had dirty minds. Shame.

Variations:

Hot Stiff One: For you ladies. Made exactly the same way.
Jameson Creamed Himself Substitute Jameson Irish Whiskey
Pinch My Bottom: Substitute Dimple Pinch Scotch Whiskey for Irish Whiskey.

WARM CREAMY NUT

1/2 shot Frangelico   *Splash of coffee*
1/2 shot Irish cream

A take-off of the Warm Creamy Bush, but these things do happen. In a rocks glass, pour Frangelico and Irish cream, then add coffee.

WARM GORILLA SNOT

1/2 shot Galliano   *Splash 151-proof rum*
1/2 shot Irish cream

Hmmm. Just the name alone puts you in that drinking mood. With a name like that it's got to be good. It worries me to know there's someone running around out there who named a drink after a monkey's nasal drainage. It worries me even more that some world traveler tasted this combination and said "tastes exactly like gorilla not." Some people are so experienced, they scare me. Pour ingredients into a shot glass. Light it. Shoot it down.

WATERFALL

1 shot peppermint schnapps   *1 shot glass of beer*

Probably the messiest shot around. This is a drink you practice at home before ordering at a bar. Fill one shot glass with peppermint schnapps and another with beer. Adjust the shot glasses in your fingers so that you place the shot of peppermint schnapps against your mouth and the shot of beer is placed above it. Pour the peppermint schnapps into your mouth in such a way that the shot of beer pours slowly into the other shot glass underneath and then into your mouth. A diagram is needed for this.

WATERMELON

2/3 shot Devotion Vodka   *1/3 shot melon liqueur*
1 shot orange juice

This can be a shot or cocktail, depending on your mood. Pour ingredients into a set up glass full of ice. Shake and strain in an up glass full of ice. For a shot, shake and strain into a shot glass.

WEDDING CAKE

1/2 shot gin   *1/2 shot amaretto*
Splash of orange juice, pineapple juice, and half & half

Tastes just like real wedding cake. Now you won't have to crash the party. Blend and serve in a fiesta glass. Great for celebrating weddings and divorces.

WEDGIE

1/2 shot Devotion Vodka   *1/2 shot Southern Comfort*
1/2 shot orange juice   *1/2 shot cranberry juice*
Float 151 -proof rum

You won't be feeling very comfortable after a few of these, if you're feeling anything at all. Invented on a slow evening when my underwear was heading north. In a set up glass full of ice, add vodka, Southern Comfort, orange juice and cranberry juice. Shake and strain into an up glass. Pour a float of 151. Drink and become numb.

WEEK AT THE BEACH

1/2 shot Devotion Vodka   *1/2 shot Southern Comfort*
1/2 shot orange juice   *1/2 shot cranberry juice*

Often confused with Sex on the Beach, basically because one leads to the other. This is a cocktail for the major vacation, or for one who never wants to go home. Pour into a set up glass full of ice. Shake, strain and serve in an up glass.

WHAT MELONS

2/3 shot Jägermeister   *1/3 shot melon liqueur*

My, what melons you have! Blame whatever you say or do on the booze. This shot is a good excuse. Pour Jager and melon liqueur into a shot glass. I promise you the melon liqueur cuts the taste of the Jager, but not the effects.

What Melons

WHITE JAMAICAN

1/2 shot rum   *1/2 shot Kahlua*
1 shot half & half

The name confuses me, but the taste makes up for any uncertainty. Pour ingredients into highball with ice.

WHITE NUN

Steamed milk   *1/3 shot brandy*
1/3 shot coffee liqueur   *1/3 shot Frangelico*

Let's hope she can still wear white when the night is over. Fill a fiesta glass with steamed milk. Add brandy, coffee liqueur and Frangelico.

WHITE OUT (SHOOTER)

1/2 shot peppermint schnapps   *1/2 shot Irish cream*

After one of these, you'll black out. Perfect for erasing a night's work. Serve chilled in a shooter glass.

WHITE RUSSIAN

2/3 shot Devotion Vodka   *1 shot half & half*
1/3 shot coffee liqueur

This is a foo-foo drink that tastes like chocolate milk but will kill brain cells faster than any sugar buzz. These will sneak up on you because you'll gulp them down like a kid drinking his Nestle's. In a highball full of ice, pour vodka, coffee liqueur, and half & half layered on top.

WHY NOT?

1/2 shot gin   *1/2 shot apricot brandy*
Dash dry vermouth and lemon juice

There's not a good reason, so what the hey. Shake and strain into a martini glass.

WILD CANADIAN GOOSE SHOT DOWN WHILE FLYING OVER AMES, IOWA

1/3 shot Yukon Jack   *1/3 shot apricot brandy*
1/3 shot Wild Turkey   *Splash orange juice*

I think the person who invented this had a bigger problem than that goose. Pour into a set up glass full of ice. Shake, strain and serve in an up glass. For the Honking Wild Canadian Goose, add a shot of vodka.

Wild Canadian Goose...

WILD FLING

1 shot wildberry schnapps *1 shot pineapple juice*
Splash cranberry juice

If you're going to have a fling, well it might as well be a wild one. This'll make you play with your wild thing. Pour ingredients into a shaker glass. Shake and strain into an up glass.

WILD ORCHID

1/2 shot Malibu Caribbean Rum *1/2 shot Devotion Vodka*
1/2 shot pineapple juice *1/2 shot cranberry juice*

Given to me by a Malibu Caribbean Rum distributor in Southern California. A great tasting shot, even if he does say so himself. Serve in a set up glass over ice. Drink and be free.

WINDEX

1/3 shot Devotion Vodka   *1/3 shot blue curacao*
1/3 shot peppermint schnapps

I designed this shot with some customers at the Fillmore Grill in San Francisco because we loved the color of Blue Shots, but we had to so something about that God-awful taste. Pour into a set up glass full of ice. Shake and strain into and up glass. You'll think your windows are dirty because you'll have difficulty seeing.

WINE COOLER

3/4 glass of white or red wine   *1/4 glass 7-Up*

A refreshing drink that tastes better home made versus those store bought imitations. Pour either red or white wine over ice in a set-up glass. Then add 7-Up and garnish with a twist.

WOO WOO

2/3 shot Devotion Vodka   *1/2 shot cranberry juice*
1/3 shot peach schnapps

I don't know if this was meant to be a train or an obnoxious guy admiring a gorgeous woman. This shot is very popular because it tastes good and people have fun ordering it, and later it's the only thing they can pronounce. Pour into a set up glass full of ice. Shake and strain into an up glass.

XYZ

2/3 shot rum   Splash of sweet & sour mix
1/3 shot triple sec

When you run out of ideas for drink names... Shake and strain into a rocks glass.

YEAST INFECTION

1/3 shot Irish cream   1/3 shot Devotion Vodka
1/3 shot amaretto   1 shot half & half

Great to drink with bread. Makes you forget life's little problems. Pour ingredients into blender. Blend and pour into fiesta glass. Then see a doctor.

YELLOW BIRD

Shot of rum   1/2 shot Galliano
Dash of creme de banana
Splash orange juice, pineapple juice and lemon juice

Poor Tweety. Too much liquid and not enough shake after going #1? Blend ingredients and serve in a fiesta glass.

YELLOW SNOW

1/2 shot Devotion Vodka   *1/2 shot Galliano*

Never drink yellow snow, unless you're into that. Pour ingredients into rocks glass full of crushed ice.

YELLOW SUBMARINE

2/3 shot rum   *1/3 shot Orange Curacao*
Splash sweet & sour mix

Now we know what made their submarine so yellow. Serve ingredients over ice in a highball.

YUKA-YUKA'S

Tequila   *Grapefruit pieces*
Orange and lemon slices   *Sugar*
Strawberries

Another one of those party punches. This one leads to raids by the police and complaints from the neighbors. Pour tequila into a large container of sliced oranges, lemons, grapefruits, strawberries and ice. Add a tablespoon of sugar for every half-gallon serving.

Z-28

1/3 shot white creme de menthe   *1/3 shot tequila*
1/3 shot creme de banana

Obviously a Chevrolet company drink. Shake and strain into a rocks glass.

ZIMA PUNCH

1 shot Zima Malt liquor   *1/2 shot cranberry juice*
1/2 shot orange juice   *Float Grand Marnier*

Refreshing, but if you're up running to the bathroom all night, I warned you. Pour ingredients into a tall glass with ice.

ZIPPER

1/3 shot Irish cream   *1/3 shot Grand Marnier*
1/3 shot tequila

Helps lube the zipper to make it easier to undo. Layered in that order in a pony glass.

YES, MASTER . . .
I WILL DRINK . . .

ZOMBIE

1 shot rum
1/2 shot creme de noyaux
1/2 shot triple sec
1/2 shot orange juice

1/2 shot pineapple juice
Splash sweet & sour mix
Splash orange curacao
Float of 151 -proof rum

You'll feel like a half dead man walking in the tropics. Basically pretty close to a Mai Tai with a 151 float. In a set up glass with ice, pour a 1/2 shot of rum, 1/2 shot each of creme de noyaux and triple sec, OJ and pineapple juice Add a splash of sweet & sour mix and splash of orange curacao. Shake and strain into a set up glass. Float a layer of 151 on top and garnish with a cherry.

Guide to Bar Etiquette

INTRODUCTION

So you want to go out for a cocktail?

Maybe you're hungry and crave a burger and a beer at the bar? Perhaps, you desire more and ask a date out for dinner. You enjoy a night out on the town. You stop by the local watering hole where you've been before. "They love me here," you say. Well, do they really?

As you open the door and walk in, the big question is, have you been a good customer? Are you someone that they are happy to see and genuinely welcome back? Or were you some kind a naughty nightmare, a huge pain in the bottom? Were you the object of late night ridicule and jokes between the staff? Is it affection they feel when they see you approaching or is it nausea? Are they welcoming you back because they honestly enjoyed your company last time you were in, or are they performing one heck of an Academy Award winning acting job and instead thinking of what they can do to your soup or drink. They might not be honestly welcoming you back but instead are wishing that you'd get a job transfer, go to AA, or go home with a transvestite (for the comedy of it all.)

Well, welcome to Bar Etiquette - *an oxymoron if there ever was one. Bar etiquette is something that until now wasn't taught but needs to be learned. The good guests, the ones that know the tricks of the trade, that know how to*

conduct themselves while slowly raising their blood alcohol level have most likely had the luxury of past employment as a bartender or waitress. It was from there that they learned how to behave in a drinking establishment. From that educational employment they nurtured their skills to impress the staff at their favorite hangout. This book was not written for them. They most likely, unless they've drank away all memory and have forgotten everything past the age of 21, already possess the proper skills and etiquette needed. They most likely don't need these instructions, but they're more than invited to read away and laugh out loud at the inexperienced ones that this book was written for.

Now for the rest of you, the amateur drinkers, the ones who cause the personnel to be manically depressed when you walk in the door or sit in their section, who think that the staff is there at your beck and call. You really do believe that slogan that "the customer is always right." You're the one who believes that the bartender really enjoys your wit and stories, knows that all the women love you, and admires how well you can handle your alcohol. Sure, the bartender just can't wait to buy you drinks all night. Well, I am sorry to say, you are extremely mistaken. You have been crazy and disillusioned for quite a long time. You either drank away way too many brain cells or were born with some form of thinking deficiency. A couple of cocktails and a little social atmosphere and you lose whatever mental, as well as physical controls you ever had. You may think of yourself as the life of the bar, but you may be looked at as the alcoholic anti-Christ - devil child. Blaming your actions on the booze gets a tad old after a while, and a good tip doesn't conceal your problems (well I guess that depends on how big the tip).

Now this is no fault of your own. You are not to blame if every time you mosey into a drinking establishment you immediately transgress back to nursery school and need a spanking (although who doesn't need or want a good spanking?). It is your lack of tutoring that causes you to naturally change from a mature adult outside a bar into a drunken ten year-old on Viagra inside a bar? Don't blame it on yourself if after a few cocktails you lose all control of bodily functions and social consciousness. They didn't teach bar behavior in night classes or Special Ed, so let's blame it on the system.

Do you need this book?

Do you really require professional guidance to develop proper bar etiquette? If you have to ask, trust me, the answer is yes. Tired of hearing the dreaded number "86?" Can you remember a time or two you got a little nasty with a cocktail waitress? Ever received an evil stare from the bartender when you yelled his name? Ever have a bouncer grab you by the neck, especially when you don't think you did anything?

IF SO START READING. *You can use the help. We are not here to make fun of the socially inept, we are here to help you. We want to educate. Humor is great, but it's high time the jokes are not at your expense. This book wasn't written so that bar staffs around the country could laugh at their problem customer (OK, maybe a little bit). Bar employees joke and tell their war stories at the end of the night and you might be a dreaded subject matter. The worse of it is, you might not even know it. So why take a chance?*

Read away and surprise that bartender about the new you.

Now don't think that since you once dated a bartender or waitress means you know what's going on, *because you don't. For one, you got* *special treatment because you gave special treatment. And two, you probably weren't the only one (sorry, the truth hurts). To be realistic, you need this book even more. You have been spoiled and you are now completely disillusioned. No more yelling at your man the bartender and demanding free drinks because you're going home with him. Fighting with him at the bar isn't really acceptable late night behavior. So sit down and learn. Impress them while you're still dating, and if I know bartenders you better hurry.*

Now don't forget, in a bar it is the bartender who is the appointed social director. *A bartender is like no other professional. Get on their good grace, and you're in good shape. You'll be able to enjoy yourself freely. Get on their bad side and forget it. Your cocktail quality, service and love life will be forever ruined. That bar will never become your official home away from home. Say or do the wrong thing (and believe me there are plenty of things you'd never think about) and you'll never be warmly welcomed back, if let back in at all.*

Oh, I know there are worse things than never getting a drink in a bar *- castration or monk hood come to mind. And there might be other bars you can go to. But if you don't learn the proper etiquette now, then you're going to just annoy the daylights out of the staff at the next place you happen to wander in to. Sooner or later you'll be out of bars to go to and your social life will consist of house parties, athletic clubs and supermarkets.*

So it is obvious that the work needs to be done. *The information is here. Read and learn. We're here to help. The guide is yours to learn and adhere to. What follows is an in depth list of what not to do. From that, unless you've destroyed every last remaining brain cell, you'll be able to surmise what you should do. You will then understand proper bar etiquette. Those that can learn the proper bar etiquette must do it before it's too late. It's probably already too late, but let's give it a try anyway. There is a chance you can be saved. Think of this as a bible and going to a bar is going to church - you eat and drink at both.*

Some of you will never change. *Some enjoy a good confrontation. You live off heckling, agitating, and pestering. You are the kind of person who enjoys some weird things: jock itch, sunburn, cold toilet seats. Some of life's real* *pleasures. You cause employees to keep changing jobs to get away from you, but you always find them. Well this book is not for you. You will probably not get anything from it, except for some great new ideas on how to torture that poor bartender. You will spend eternity in bar hell, where you will be placed as a service bartender in a tourist hotel making fresh fruit blended daiquiris. Then you'll know real bar hell.*

What is the perfect customer? *Well, we'd love everybody to order a beer and a shot, stay clean and quiet, tip like a maniac, look like a model, and go home with the staff. But let's not be that selfish. We do understand that you've had a hard day or a long week. You need to let loose some stress.*

You need to forget your problems in the outside world. *You want someone to get you a drink, prepare your meal, clean up after you. Sounds great, but we're not your mother. Nowhere in our job description does it say we have to "baby-sit the bad drunk."*

This is our office. *Would you like it if we showed up at your work, took a seat in your office, threw napkin balls at you to get your attention, drank shots, drooled on your desk, hit on your receptionist, and demanded free insurance or stock? I didn't think so. So read and learn the guidelines we have set forth.*

There are many different types of bartenders, *all with their own talents and egos. Some treat the bar like their castle, some can't wait to close up and go home (theirs or someone else's home.) Some bartenders love the mere presence behind a bar. They feel like an actor on stage putting on a show. A tip is their ovation for a great performance. Other bartenders would rather be back in bed. They do it to pay the rent and support some expensive habit they might have accidentally picked up over the years. And then there is the bartender with an ego the size of their liver. They think of the bar as heaven and they are the almighty, in total control of your social life. They might be right, but they want to prove it.*

Then there is the bartender with a hangover. *An animal with no human qualities, and I'm not talking about the daytime bartender who had a long night. He expected his punishment. I'm talking about the nighttime bartender* who had a long night, morning, and afternoon. At times their head has barely touched the pillow-if it touched at all. The pain and agony they feel will be directly aimed at you, as if it is your fault. With them, you can do no right. Be quiet, get your order right and sit back and watch the show, especially if his girlfriend who hasn't seen him all night comes in to get some answers. At these times the bar should raise drink prices for the entertainment value.

So it is clear that every bartender and waitress will have his or her own pet peeves. What will instantly cause a nervous breakdown with one bartender won't mean a thing to another. What one waiter will think is funny, might cause another to wet his pants. What gets a smile from one bouncer could get a steroid rush from another. So it is better to be safe than sorry. Memorize the don'ts and just don't do them.

Just as bartenders are not alike, not all bars are alike. There are different types of bars that require a much different type of behavior. You'd make quite an impression ordering a Chi Chi at the local Irish tavern, yet picking a fight with the person next to you won't go over too well at the beach front resort bar. I wouldn't recommend asking for a "dirty vodka martini, stirred with two olives in a chilled martini glass" at a down and dirty, beer smelling college bar where the drinks are served in plastic cups. However you probably can't urinate in the corner and throw up on yourself at too many trendy, expensive restaurant bars. It's a fair assumption to make that the acceptable noise you can make and the blood alcohol level you are allowed is inversely proportional to the amount of clothing the bartender wears. What you can get away with at "Coyote Ugly" is a lot more than any place where the bartenders wear a bow tie and white jacket.

So if you enjoy a good bar scene, this book is for you. Common sense will get you far (or to put it correctly- no common sense will get you far away), but you need the experience and bar knowledge this book will provide.

The following has been put together from many years of bartending as well as many nights playing customer.

There have been countless hours of observation and analysis. It has not been for entertainment that I planted myself on a barstool and begun the necessary surveillance. Oh, of course one or two libations were hoisted in the process, I didn't want to seem out of place. And a little flirting here and there never hurt anyone. And there might have been nights that were completely blacked out and I don't know where the heck I was the next morning, but it was all in the name of research.

So where do we start?

BAR FOULS

The Obvious: The fastest and easiest way to get kicked out

The Obvious: The fastest and easiest way to get kicked out of a bar or any establishment. Try any of these when you just really want to get a friendly escort through the front door in a hurry. A nice picture of you will be printed as "Least Wanted" in the employee break room. You'll definitely get your name permanently etched on the 86'd list. We shouldn't even have to put these in, except that they do happen and they sure are funny.

Grab a waitresses' bottom. I told you these were the obvious. The waitress is thought of as either a little sister or a wild fantasy (or dream come true) for the bartender. You don't want to get mixed into either.

Stealing Tips: Stealing is naughty. ***You go to jail, then, get raped, beaten....***

Stealing from a bartender is worse.

Fighting: Steroids and alcohol just don't mix.

Sleeping out at the bar. Unless you're really, really tired and don't snore loud or drool. Drooling at the bar alone is a big no-no.

Throwing up on yourself. Unless you don't hit anyone else and it doesn't stink and there's none of those chunky pieces.

Do drugs. Just learn to say no, or you brought enough for everyone

Dine and Dash: Just don't be the slowest person in the group.

Don't tip. If you really believe "you earn a tip," tell that to the guy you just stiffed. When you don't tip a bartender or waitress, they think of it as you didn't pay for their having to kiss your $%&@* ass all night. Usually it's the biggest pains in there customer that tips the least.

Sneak in your own alcohol. If you can't afford to buy a drink at a bar, drink at home. Especially don't be dumb enough to walk in with your own beer that the bar doesn't serve.

Don't bitch about a hangover. It's something to be proud of.

Speaking of hangovers....

BARTENDER

Bartender can be your best friend or your worst nightmare.

It might be true that the customer is always right, but don't forget that it is the bartender who decides who will be the customers.

Don't spill a drink and then ask for another. **This is not Baskin and Robbins and you've dropped your ice cream scoop. It's time you face up to your own actions. Clean your own mess and buy another drink without saying a word.**

No preaching at the bar. *We'll do the preaching.*

No baby talk. **Most bartenders don't understand or have patience for kids, so please don't act or talk like one.**

No baby pictures. **See above. We could fake like we are really excited about your pictures, but manic depression sets in too quickly.**

Order a drink one drink at a time. **Bartenders just love the exercise** going back and forth to get your drinks one at a time, and the other customers just love the wait.

Take your drinks **to the table before you pay.**

Drop your money for payment into a puddle of beer. (**Don't even say that the baa is messy, and it's our job to clean the bar.**) As a matter of fact, **never tell us what any aspect of our job is.**

Recognize good service *when given.*

Remember to say "Please," "Thank You," "Come home with me."

Want to buy a person a drink **and expect us to know what the heck they are drinking.**

Do not bitch if you think you have been waiting too long. **Do not bitch because you missed last call. Do not bitch because your beer is too warm. Make that no bitching about anything.**

"God damn it, where's the bartender?" - **God damn it, where's your baby-sitter?**

Don't celebrate your 21st birthday at the bar **you've been going to for years. It makes us feel guilty.**

Not being ready **when it's your turn to order at a busy bar.**

Don't step up to the bar and try to get the attention of the bartender *unless you* know what you want. We have time for many things, but watching you make up your mind just doesn't top the list.

Make sure you know what your whole order is *before you get the bartender's attention.*

Don't try and impress a bartender, **like how much you can drink, how much money you have** Nothing impresses us, except maybe a great **boob job.**

Don't be a wine expert *at the bar.*

Don't try and change a bartender's attitude. *It's that way for a reason.*

In a sports bar, **don't root for the opposing team of a city you're in. This is one of the main reasons for bar brawls and the staff will probably jump in against you.**

"Why don't you use fresh OJ and Grapefruit?"

-**Why don't you go to the store and buy it and cut it and squeeze it yourself.**

Don't order a drink and then turn your back **and talk to someone behind you. We don't have the energy to get your attention the way you try and get ours.**

When you get the attention of one bartender, don't say, *"Only that bartender can make it the way I like it."*

Chewing tobacco. **There's not a person in the world who understands your habit and doesn't mind cleaning a glass with that residue of a gross, disgusting mess.**

The number of ingredients **in a person's drink is indirectly proportional to their IQ.**

It's a busy night and a customer **is waving like there's no tomorrow, which is bad enough. Then, he orders 2 cokes and a water. If you want water, go to the sink in the bathroom. If you want a coke, go to a movie.**

Asking for tea, **unless it's a Long Island.**

Ask for fresh coffee. **Fresh is within the same day. Asking for decaf coffee. -What is this Starbucks? "Do you have a cappuccino machine?" -In a bar?**

Remember the rule, **no breakfast drinks after lunchtime ends (Bloody Mary's, Fizz Drinks or Starssckc specials).**

Customers who demand an event on TV **without care for others. Then, they only drink water or coffee or don't even watch.**

Don't be those that come for the free ride *(happy hours, no cover, free buffets)*

No crying about an ex being at the bar. **We'd never make it through a shift if we worried about ex's showing up.**

Guy in the well trying to talk to you when you are busy. **Or the "Hey do you have a second?" -Sure, you other 200 people, let me hear poor Bob's life story and how virgin Bill finally got laid.**

Don't be a girl that tries to get drinks for free **They have no problem paying for items at the mall, shoe store, hair salon. Why at a bar? They think a little flirting or smooching will get their drinks for free. Well you know what, it does!**

Someone orders a gin and tonic *for a person they are with.*

Drink is served and paid for by the friend. Person drinking it says, "Don't order gin and tonic," then asks, "Is there Tanqueray in here?"

-Yeah, I read your mind.

"I want to buy a round." Then disappear. Or you don't have enough money.

Guys want to buy girls a drink. Girls accept. *The girls still* **don't want to talk to them, so the guys don't think they should have to pay for the drinks. Tuff $#!+. You lost. The bar doesn't lose. We get the money and the humor of watching you strike out.**

Asking for aspirin. **Have a shot to get rid of any head or body pains.**

"I'll get you next time," **when not tipping. -Yeah, sure you will buddy. I'll get you next time too.**

"That drink wasn't good, can I have another?" **Or "Can I have something else?" First, never criticize a bartender's drink. Second, if you didn't like my first drink, guaranteed you're not going to like the second.**

Use proper order. **Not "OJ and vodka." The alcohol is called first.**

Don't talk too fast, **too softly, mumble, or expect us to know your sign language.**

"Will you save our seats?" **"Will you watch our coats?"** -Sure, we can baby sit some nights also.

No bad toupees, **extra wonder bras, or women with hairy armpits.**

When one guy orders for the group, **and one of the drinks comes back as being wrong. Then he expects a free replacement. Wrong. You** made the mistake. (Rule #1 of bartender's mistakes: If the customer ordered wrong, learn to like that drink.)

Don't send your friend a strong shooter, **and not willing to do one yourself. Wimpy behavior is not tolerated.**

Please, no bar aerobics **while trying to get the bartender's attention - no jumping, the two arm wave, whistling, running down bar, or anything to break a sweat trying to get the attention of the bartender who's probably ignoring you anyway.**

Don't sing along to juke box or CD. This is not a Karaoke bar.

If it is a Karaoke bar that you're in, then this whole book probably doesn't make sense to you.

Do not Promote your club in other clubs. **Handing out your fliers or gift certificates to promote yourself?!?, It's called customer stealing and expect strong retribution.**

Don't take it out on the staff **if some girl you thought "was yours" leaves with some other guy, especially if it's one of the staff that left with her.**

Know your drink: **Margaritas have salt unless you ask for no salt. Martinis are made from gin unless you order vodka, Irish Coffees are topped with whipped cream unless you ask for no whipped cream.**

"Can I get a screaming tornado?"
-Sure, what's in it? "I don't know."

"Can you get me a taxi?" **-Sure, I have time. Why don't I just drive you home real quick?**

Order an expensive vodka, **then use OJ and Peach Schnapps as a mixer.**

Don't ask for change. Buy something or leave the whole bill as a tip.

Don't point out your ideas of imperfections with the bar. Don't be the perfect consultant. "That light bulb is out. You should paint this place... You know what you guys should do?"-You know what you should do, open your own bar.

Never argue with your bartender. Imagine that you are ten years old and the bartender is your mother and father. If you argue, you will be punished.

Always follow a bartender's advice, **no matter how silly it sounds.**

Know your BAR LINGO. Do you want it up or over? -"Up or over what?" A drink served tall, with no ice, or the garnish on the side doesn't mean more drink.

"I want the coldest beer you got." -I'll get right on measuring the temperature of all of them.

"How come you're closing, you're supposed to be open till 2am?" -It is 1:55.

Wave, yell for bartender's attention, then when we get to you, you turn to your friends and get your order ready.

"It's my birthday, can I have a free drink?" -Well, I don't recall receiving anything from you on my birthday.

Don't whistle at a bartender. Whistle at your dog or girlfriend, but not at a bartender

Most bartenders hate serving food, so eat at home and bring your own water.

Don't go into bar and ask the bartender where's a good place to go.

*Don't say, "Make me something good." -****Everything we make is good.***

"Do I get a free drink?" Or, "You're charging me?" -I'm sorry.

This is a business, it's not a charity. We are not here to give away cocktails to the needy.

When bartender asks what you want, don't say, "Surprise me." -"OK, I'll shave my crotch."

Don't say, "Smile." We smile when and at our own discretion.

Don't hand over crumpled money.

.250 change on order, don't say, "Keep it." If it's a cheap tip, don't announce it.

Do not leave a drink, it gets picked up, then demand another. If your car gets stolen or you crash it, do you go back to the dealer and ask for a new car?

No humping at the bar, **unless we're next.** Don't mumble, especially if you are sober. *Don't hug a bartender* **if you are a guy.**

Don't hug them if you're a girl and your date is bigger than them.

"What do you have?" - What your girlfriend had last night.

Drink whores: Girls that talk to someone just to get a free drink.

Don't ask a bartender, **"What else do you do?"**

Do not double order from two different bartenders. If you ordered them, they make them, then you pay for them.

DO NOT ADD-ON: "Oh, one more thing.

DO NOT ASK, "Can I trade this in for something else?"-Yeah, didn't you see the car on the window.

DON 'T SCREAM. There is a direct reverse correlation between a girl who makes noise in a bar and one that makes noise in the bedroom.

"There's no alcohol in here." - Did you do a chemical evaluation?

"This Chi Chi has no alcohol." If you like the taste of alcohol, don't order a milk shake.

Have the money ready. Don't look at the bartender with a puzzled expression when he says, "That'll be $5."

If you're HAMMERED, THAN K the bartender for cutting you off. Because he certainly could be making more money by serving you (you

would have no idea how much money you gave him.)

Don't say, "I gave you a twenty." -If the bartender says it was a ten, it was a ten.

If you embarrass yourself and the people you are with when you drink and you are an obvious amateur drinker, then only drink on New Year's Eve and St. Paddy's Day. Those are your national holidays and you'll be in good company.

No cheap perfume or cologne.

If you have one of those high- pitched, screeching voices, **have someone else do the ordering.**

"Hey, hey, hey!" What are you, a horse?

Yelling "Hey, hey you" will create a high level of dislike between you and "You".

Don't snap your fingers.

If you just turned 21, please practice drinking at home before you go out.

Male patrons don't hit on female bartenders, though the opposite is true for female patrons hitting on male bartenders.

Put a napkin or coaster on your drink when leaving your seat. That is the sign you are coming back. Don't ask the bartender to watch it for you. The bartender is not your guardian angel of drinks, seats, purses, sweaters, dates...

Don't say, "Make it strong." Order a double and pay for it.

When you've had enough (this is usually the case when your cheek and ear are propped up against the floor) cut yourself off.

Remember the rule: The louder the bang of your dice cup, the smaller the bang in your pants.

When you spill a drink, offer to clean it up. The bartenders most likely will do it themselves, but the offer is noticed.

The bartender sees and hears all. How you relate to other customers will affect the bartender's judgment of your character. This relates to the speed of service you will receive and the quality of product you will obtain.

Don't put your belongings on the chair **next to you if the bar is busy.**

Don't complain about a drink after you've finished half of it. Better yet, don't complain about a drink.

Never ask a bartender **"When are you going to get a real job?" He'll ask, "When are you going to get a real social skill?"**

No dumping unwanted shots on the floor (or in plants, vases, other people's drinks...)

"It's his birthday, aren't you going to buy him a drink?" **The** bartender will buy someone a drink when they are good and ready, and when they feel the person deserves it. Any ways, it's your frien why don't you buy them a drink?
Don't exchange a drink when it is your screw-up. "My friend

ordered me this, but I don't want it. Can I get a instead?" You're not the most important person in the bar.

*If the bartender is talking to **someone else, wait your turn.** Have enough money for your order.*

If you order a drink by accident, and the bartender makes it, it is yours to pay for and drink unless you have one heck of a guy back there or you've made a real great impression.

My brother is the mayor of Lafayette!"
-What's Lafayette? In anything.

Don't come into a bar already hammered.

Cigarette smokers. Especially those chain smokers who create a butt mountain on and around the ashtray.

"Do you accept checks?" - No! "Well it's all I have."-Well then, it's all you're going to have.

Don't get upset at the bartender for following the rules placed on him by the management. Make a great first impression on your bartender, because that impression will last all night and will determine how he serves you.

Don't do the pasting your money or credit card on your forehead trick to get the bartender's attention

Don't tell the bartender how to do his job. He dsesn't come into your office every Monday morning and tell you how you can be a better stockbroker. Just because you recognize the bartender, don't pxpect him to recognize you. You may have been in the bar five weeks ago and he was the one bartender you met there, but he has met a gazillion people since then and has killed a gazillion brain cells since then, and there is a good chance he might not remember you.

Don't ask for the beer selection more than once, **eepeclally when it's listed in front of you.**

Do not close out a credit card tab, **and then order more.**

Don't be the last table that won't leave at closing.

*Don't pull out a handful of ones **and expect us to count it.***

Do not hand over a handful of $1 bills, we have to count them, and it's always too short.

Don't say, "Can I get?" -No. I'll get it for you.

Can I order a "Zombie's Nipple?" - What is that? "It's the house drink at the saloon down the street.

-Great. Then go down the street and order it.

*Don't ask the bartender **"What do I want?"***

Guys don't order drinks like Champagne Cocktails.

Don't hate the bartender for following local and state laws. If you don't have ID, it sure the hell isn't the bartenders fault.

Don't burp at the bar. Even if we didn't hear it, we probably felt it.

Don't do drugs then show it at the bar.

Stutterers. Get someone else to order for you.

Don't complain about prices. Don't go behind the bar.

Don't try and cash a check. Don't ask to borrow money.

*Don't ask to run a tab **and pay later.***

Don't' get hammered and leave your credit card.

*Don't throw things at the bartenders **to get their attention.***

Don't throw things at other customers. Throw things at yourself only.

Don't order virgin drinks.

*Don't sneeze at the bar **and not cover up.***

Don't say, "There's no alcohol in here!"

Don't accuse the bartender of under pouring. Worry more that he's going to get you wasted.

Don't order one drink at a time and make the bartender make one drink at a time.

Do not offer to buy a drink for someone and not want to pay for it or walk away.

"You're just a bartender." -You're worse. You're just a customer.

Don't promise sex to get past the door or for a drink (unless you really mean it.)

"Can we have some more peanuts? Pretzels? Anything free?" -Sure, help yourself with the furniture.

One drink wonders (person who has one drink all night at prime bar space.)

If you're not 21, ***don't beg.***

Don't flirt with the bartender all night then at the end of the night go home with someone else.

"Hook me up. We'll take care of you." -Great, you'll pay my rent when I get fired.

Ordering drinks incorrectly, for example, "May I have a Vodka Stoli."?

Don't order a drink then decide you don't like it and ask for something else. It's time you learn to be responsible for your own actions.

When people ask you to leave their jackets and belongings behind the bar. Then ask every ten seconds if they can get something out of their bag.

If you're friends with the bartender and you come in and ask for free drinks all night long. What if we come into your office and ask for free stocks or real estate all day long?

"Where is it fun tonight?" If you have to ask, then you are Mr. Personality.

Don't change your order after I've begun the process of making it. Not just after I've begun making it, but after a bartender has begun the process in his mind. And after a long night the night before, that process might be quite a while.

*Do not go to a bar with a cold **and cough all over everybody.***

Never, under any circumstances, complain that your drink is too strong. It is the fastest way to forever lose respect from the bartender

Don't grab your own straw, napkin, garnish, or anything that breaks the bartenders rhythm. If you want a job, apply.

*Don't drink other peoples' drinks **without their permission.***

Bathe (see "Foreigners".)

No directing traffic (hey, this person needs a drink).

Person orders large order, all well liquor except call for himself. In other words, don't look cheap, even if you are.

"Don't you know who I am?" -Yeah, some guy who thinks he's going to get special service.

Don't use the bartender to get your husband jealous! Unless he's not going to find out. If you're married and want to sleep with the bartender, please, please, please leave the ring at home!

Don't think taking the bartender home will give you special treatment next time. Well, you might as well give that one a try.

"I'll take what that bartender made me earlier." - **Well if** you don't know what it was, go to that bartender from earlier.

"I'll have the same." Or, "She'll have the same." -Don't test our memories. We've spent many evenings destroying it.

"Hey, where's Paul, the customer who was here last night?" -I swear people ask that.

Don't pay with coins. Leave your piggy bank at home.

"Hey, do you remember me?" -No, you have to pay for your drink.

Pick your nose at the bar, **or table, or anywhere.**

"I didn't order this." **(Usually a woman) -No. Your date did for you. Bitch at him.**

Trying to get one more drink at two O'clock AM.

When bartender empties a bottle, there's always 1 customer who shouts, "Hey, isn't the drink free?"

Men who don't order for the woman first.

*Large groups that order and pay individually, **especially with credit cards.***

One drink credit card orders.

Don't cancel order after bartender has begun to make it.

Whiny customers. If there is a problem, don't revert back to being 10 years old.

Don't tell your life stories or expect the bartender to be your psychotherapist, and no bad jokes. We will give you a charity laugh, but we'll also give you the worse advice on life, sometimes on purpose.

Don't throw out a gazillion drink order and expect us to remember it. We have the worst memories. If we can't remember what we did last night, how in the heck is there a chance we'll remember your drink order?

"I'll have a Long Island Iced Tea, and make it strong." Any drink loaded with booze "and make it strong" is a proof that you are an amateur at drinking. For that matter, any time someone says "and make it strong" makes us want to put a little foreign object in your "strong" cocktail. The only thing worse is to complain that your drink is too strong.

Do not order "a vodka/tonic" and complain about the vodka. Ask what the well is if you're going to be rude later.

-**What can I get you? "What do you have?"** *-Well, let's start with the A's. in other words, don't make us recite the drink ABC's.*

Guys that like to show off that $100 bill. *Especially the guys that show it off and then pay with a $5 bill.*

Do not comment: "I'm never coming back here again." *That comment excites bartenders and waiters and they want you to follow through on that promise.*

When someone wants to buy you a drink *(especially the house) and you order the most expensive thing.*

Correct way to order. *Have money on the bar, and be patient.*

When the bar is two or three people deep, *do not wave in back of them trying to get your order first.*

Have your order ready *when you get the bartender's attention.* **No coffee drinks in the summer.**

No blended drinks in the winter.

"This is a great place to build a bar." -Boy, that line sure is a new one.

Know your pronunciation of what you order. "I'll have an *Almarando." That's Amaretto.*

"What do you have in a bottle?" -Mustard, Ketchup, A-1...

"This is on my buddy."- *Great, congratulations, should I go find him?*

"Are you open?" *-No, I work the shift when we're closed. I also wear this apron when I'm off.*

Loud talking. *We'll do the talking.*

Loud laughter. *Unless it's to my joke.* **The garnish tray is not a buffet line.**

Do not blow your nose, then put the napkin on the bar.

Don't ask for water and not tip, *or else you'll start getting charged for bottles or there will be something special in there for you.*

Don't order *when my back is turned.*

Don't order anything in a martini glass unless it's a martini

Don't fake like you're dying of thirst, or you will be. **Don't bang on the tabletop,** unless it's with your head.

No cell phones-ringing, talking.

"Do you have specials?" *"Can we still get happy hour?" Don't ask "What's your cheapest beer?" or "What do you have in a can?" If you are going to ask questions like these, ones that show the bartender that you are broke or cheap as hell, then you're a marked man in their eyes as someone to serve last (or never).*

Humping at the bar, *unless you brought enough for all of us.*

Waitresses:

"Are *you sure you work here? Aren't you a waitress?"* **-Yes, but I'm not your @#$%&* mother.**

Order a drink and then you're nowhere to be found....

Don't even bother hitting on her, **asking for a phone number, begging for a date...**

"I have a tab at the bar." **-Then get your lazy bottom up to the bar.**

Don't touch. **Touch yourself and enjoy it.**

Don't touch the tray or take drinks off it yourself.

Nothing like having the remaining glasses crashing on the floor. Also, no tickling armpits when the arm is holding a big tray full of cocktails. If it spills, I'm aiming for you.

Don't grab arms or touch legs. **Don't grab clothing, apron, ponytail, anything.**

Coffee drinkers and refill all night. Coffee drinking is OK only in the morning, unless it's an Irish Coffee obviously.

People not getting their order together.

Making the waitress come by four or five times. **-Are you ready to order? "Not yet. Haven't even looked at the menu."-Well, that's OK. Get back to the door and a hungry party will sit down."**

Guy says, "If you bring it over really quick there's a bigger tip in it for you." **-Sure. Boy can I use an extra quarter.**

One drink all night long at prime table.

"I'll have just water." -There's a garden hose outside.

Mouth to mouth talkers. When I need mouth to mouth resuscitation or a big, wet smooch I'll let you know.

People that can't control their spit when talking. Bad Breath, Both of these usually turn out to be the "mouth to mouth talkers."

Watch your cigarette, asshole, and I don't mean butt.

"Can I run a tab?" (at a busy place.) -Sorry, you're not at your country club.

"Do you have crackers or peanuts?" -No, I have a food menu. I can see this table is going to be a bunch of big spenders.

Bread and sodas at the table. **Then too full for dinner.**

Don't ask for low fat plates or non-fat substitutes. **If you go to a restaurant, plan on gaining weight.**

"Cobb salad with the dressing on the side. Make it Blue Cheese."-You might as well get a greasy cheeseburger!

Stay at the table after you finished dinner when it's busy.

No crying babies. **No crying adults.**

No sloppy tables.

Hugging. This most likely goes for all employees, but I must admit those with recent enhancements on their chest can probably hug all they want.

"Can I have my bread warmer?" -Sure, I'll put it in my pants for a few minutes

Half orders. Don't eat % of your plate then say you don't like it.

Waiter asks if you want something else, "No I'm too full." If you eat until you're full, you're paying.

AT THE DOOR

At the Door:

*When you see that large bounce
might feel. He **is a bouncer for***

"I'm sleeping with the bartender.

-Yeah, who's not.

*"I'm dating the manager." **(see bartender)***

Go into private door and say, **"I know the manager."** *"My friend is almost 21".*

"I forgot my ID" **as she's pushing up her Wonder bra.**

"Can I take my glass with me?" **when leaving. -Sure, take anything else, and try to make sure that it is also illegal.**

Don't be the loud, obnoxious customer in line.

"I shouldn't have to pay $5 to get in, **I'm going to spend $50 at the bar." -Hell, spend $45 at the bar and give me the $5.**

*"I know Randy." **-I'm Randy.***

"I just want to go in and see if my friends are here." **Or, "I just want to go inside and say hi to the bartender."** -Great, pay the $5 and go inside and say hi all night.

"I know the owner." -**I am the owner.**

"I'm a friend of Bill the manager." **-OK, what's his last name? "Huh, I don't know."**

"I know the DJ."

"I know the bartender." "I know the janitor."

"I just called. They said the cover was only $2."

-You called the wrong place.

"I know so and so." -Of course you do. Then he would have put you on the list.

"My friend is not 21, can she come in? **She's not going to drink."** *"My friends Muslim, it's against her religion to drink.*

Can she come in?"

"I'm on the guest list." -**What guest list??**

"I'm related to the owner of the other place across the street." Or, "My brother works there."-Then go there!

"Why is it $$$$ here and $$ down the street?" -Because the local college band is playing down the street.

"I know the promoter promoting this club."

"You're just the doorman." **-Wellplan on going to the club down the street.**

Cutting in line. There's a line for a reason. Do you cut in line at a bank or supermarket?

When a guy tries to impress a group of friends at the door and plays the big man scene. Then he tips $2.

Girls busting their boobies and trying to get in. This might work on the weak at heart (me), but not the seasoned professional. Though this one is OK to still try.

People that hang out too long.

The last guy the doorman has to kick out at 2am. This is usually the same guy who's been hitting on the waitress. I said guy because door guys usually don't kick out girls hitting on someone.

"I'm a friend of"... -Whoever! Does this ever work?

MAITRE D

"Oh, I'm not going to sit here. It's right by the door." -Well it's our only table. "I don't care."

-Then sit **outside the door.**

People come in for a reservation. "We'll have table 10." -Well there's somebody sitting there. "I don't care. Move them." Don't demand any table numbers. You may think you are the most person ever to step into the restaurant, but I promise, the staff there doesn't look at it the same way you do. Unless you pay.

When the place is full and you don't have a reservation: just plain lying, faking a reservation, peeking at reservation book.

They want a table, there's one available, but only for a limited time. Group says, "OK, we'll be quick." Then they take forever.

Hard to understand people on the phone. If you mumble, have someone else make the phone call.

Some one hands you a wad of bills in your hand with a handshake.

"Get us a good table."

And it turns out to be three $1 bills.

Late for reservation, then bitch because you have to wait. We sometimes have to give a table to a starving couple that's been standing patiently here while you dilly dally along getting here.

Dear Foreigners,

I know you haven't learned our customs, but it is time. No more being the brunt of many bartenders' jokes and gags. The following is a short list of things to remember, received from a number of local bartenders and cocktailers: Learn to tip. We're in America.

BAD PICKUP LINES

Do what Americans do (well most anyways).

Don't take a table for hours for smoking and not drinking, and

obviously not tipping. Learn English.

Learn our currency. Learn to drink properly.

Lose that accent so we can understand you.

Shave your armpits. (I know, they're tough out there.)

Shower. (Really tough). Quit picking up our women.

It's time we all face the facts, pick up lines don't, and hopefully never will work. But, if you must use one, for either sport or hobby, at least make sure they are an attempt to be humorous. The following is a list of some of the best (and worst) lines heard around bars across the country.

Guy: "You're the best looking girl in the bar." Girl: "I'm the only person in the bar."

You're hotter than a stove.

How do you like your eggs in the morning, fertilized or unfertilized? "You look great tonight."-What, I looked bad last night?

"Do you ever sleep?" -Sure come over to my house tonight and I'll prove it.

I have a sandpapery, cat like tongue. Want to feel?"

Your eyes look great in the night. Can I see what they look like in the morning?

I wish you were a door so I could slam you all day. Nice legs... what time do they open?

Do you work for UPS? I thought I saw you checking out my package.

You've 206 bones in your body, want one more?

I may not be the best looking guy in here, but I'm the only 'one here talking to you.

I'm a bird watcher and I'm looking for a Big Breasted Bed Thrasher: have you seen one?

I'm fighting the urge to make you the happiest woman on eannionigm. Want to play army? I'll lay down and you can blow the hell outta me.

I wish you were a Pony Carousel outside Superdrug, so I could ride you all day long for a quarter. I'd really like to see how you look when I'm naked.

Is that a ladder in your stockings or the stairway to heaven?

You might not be the best looking girl here, but beauty is only a light switch away. Are those real?

You must be the limp doctor because I've got a stiffy.

I'd walk a million miles for one of your smiles, and even farther for that thing you do with your tongue. If it's true that we are what we eat, then I could be you by morning.

Well, it's not just going to suck itself. (Look down at your crotch) You know, if I were you, I'd have sex with me.

You. Me. Whipped cream. Handcuffs. Any questions?

F@# me if I'm wrong, but is your name Sherry Titsbottom?

Those clothes would look great in a crumpled heap on my bedroom floor.

My name is (name)... remember that, you'll be screaming it later.

Do you believe in love at first sight or should I walk by again?

Hi, I'm Mr. Right. Someone said you were looking for me.

My friend wants to know if YOU think I'M cute.

Hi. The voices in my head told me to come over and talk to you. My name isn't Elmo, but you can tickle me anytime you want to. Oh, I'm sorry, I thought that was a Braille nametag.

I know milk does a body good, but DAMN, how much have you been drinking?

If you were the last woman and I was the last man on earth, I bet we could do it in public.

Wanna come over for some pizza and sex? No? Why?

Don't you like pizza?

Baby, I'm an American Express lover... you shouldn't go home without me.

Do you sleep on your stomach? Can I???

I lost my puppy. Can you help me find him? I think he went into this cheap motel room. (Lick finger and wipe on her shirt). Let's get you out of these wet clothes.

Your name must be Daisy, because I have the incredible urge to plant you right here! Roses are red, violets are blue, I like spaghetti, let's go screw.

Just call me Milk, I'll do your body good.

Your body's name must be Visa, because it's everywhere I want to be. Can I buy you a drink, or do you just want the money?

I may not be Fred Flintstone, but I bet I can make your Bed Rock.

My love for you is like the energizer bunny, it keeps going and going and going....

That shirt looks very becoming on you, but if I were on you, I'd be cumming too.

Yo, Baby, you be my Dairy Queen, I'll be your Burger King, you treat me right, and I'll do it your way right away.

I'd like to screw your brains out, but it appears that someone beat me to it.

I enjoy doing maintenance, you look like someone I would like to "tinker" around with.

I enjoy doing plumbing. You look like someone I'd like to pump.

I enjoy doing carpentry. You look like someone I'd like to hammer and nail.

I enjoy being a mason. You look like something I'd like to lay my brick on.

I enjoy being a locksmith. Your legs are something I'd like to open. You must be from Pearl Harbor, 'cause baby you're the Bomb.

If you were a new hamburger at McDonald's, you would be McGorgeous. Is that Windex? Because I can see myself in your pants.

Wanna play "house"? You be the screen door and I'll slam you all night long.

If you're going to regret this in the morning, we can sleep until the afternoon.

If you were a car, I'd wax you and ride you all over town.

Guy: "Would you like to dance?" Girl: "I don't care for this song and surely wouldn't dance with you." Guy: "I'm sorry, you must have misunderstood me, I said you look fat in those pants." Excuse me, do you have your phone number, I seem to have lost mine.

I'd look good on you.

I'd like to buy you something. How about a hotel room? I'm new in town, could I have directions to your house.

If your left leg was Thanksgiving and your right leg Christmas, can I visit you between the Holidays? You look like a girl that has heard every line in the book, so what's one more going to hurt Excuse me, do you wanna fuck, or should I apologize.

Do you want to dance? No? Well I guess a blowjob is out of the question.

Hi, I'm a necrophiliac, how good are you at playing dead? I've lost my bed, can I borrow yours?

You must be Jamaican, because Jamaican me crazy.

My recipe for love is one cup of you, one cup of me, knead till hard, and serve hot and wet.

Are your legs tired? Because you've been running through my mind all day long.

You be the tree, and I'll wrap you like a Koala.

Do you have a quarter? My mother told me to call home when I met the girl of my dreams.

The word for the night is legs, let's go back to my room and spread the word.

Hey baby, what's your sign? Caution, slippery when wet, dangerous curves ahead, yield?

Was you dad a farmer? Cause you sure have great melons.

Wanttoplayconductor?YoucanbetheengineerandI'llgoChoo-choo. You must be Jelly, cause jam don't shake like that.

Hi, my name is Skippy, like the peanut butter. I'll stick to the roof of your mouth.

Hi, my name is Pogo, want to jump on my stick?

I'm a battery, you're a bag of chips. I'm Eveready, you're free to lay (Frito-lay).

Let's get something straight between us.

"I have a lot of East Coast in me. Want some in you?"

WAYS TO TURN MEN DOWN

HE:	I'm a photographer. I've been looking for a face like yours...
SHE:	I'm a plastic surgeon. I've been looking for a face like yours.
HE:	Hi. Didn't we go on a date once? Or was it twice?
SHE:	Must've been once. I never make the same mistake twice.
HE:	How did you get to be so beautiful?
SHE:	I must've been given your share.
HE:	Will you go out with me this Saturday?
SHE:	Sorry. I'm having a headache this weekend.
HE:	Your face must turn a few heads.
SHE:	And your face must turn a few stomachs.
HE:	Go on, don't be shy. Ask me out.
SHE:	Okay, get out.
HE:	I think I could make you very happy.
SHE:	Why? Are you leaving?
HE:	What would you say if I asked you to marry me?
SHE:	Nothing. I can't talk and laugh at the same time.
HE:	Can I have your name!?
SHE:	Why? Don't you already have one?
HE:	Shall we go see a movie?
SHE:	I've already seen it.
HE:	Where have you been all my life?
SHE:	Hiding from you.
HE:	Haven't I seen you some place before?
SHE:	Yes. That's why I don't go there anymore.
HE:	Is this seat empty?
SHE:	Yes, and this one will be if you sit down.

HE: So, what do you do for a living?
SHE: I'm a female impersonator.
HE: Hey baby, what's your sign?
SHE: Do not enter.

MALE VS FEMALE

A focus group of bartenders were asked if they could nail a woman's personality based on what she drinks. Though interviewed separately, they concurred on almost all counts. The results: **Beer Personality:** *Casual, low-maintenance, down to earth. Your Approach: Challenge her to a game of pool.*

Blender Drinks Personality: *Flaky, annoying, a pain in the ass. Your Approach: Avoid her, unless you want to be her cabin boy.*

Mixed Drinks Personality: *Older, has picky taste, knows what she wants.*

Your Approach: You won't have to approach her. She'll send YOU a drink.

Wine Personality *(not including white zinfandel*):* *Conservative and classy, sophisticated.*

Your Approach: Tell her you wish Reagan had had four more years... Alzheimer's and term limits be damned. **White Zin* Personality:** *Easy, thinks she is classy and sophisticated, yet actually has no clue.*

Your approach: Make her feel smarter than she is.

Shots Personality: *Hanging with frat-boy pals or looking to get drunk... and naked. Your Approach: Easiest hit in the joint. Nothing to do but wait.*

Then, there is the male addendum. The deal with guys is it's very simple and clear cut.

Domestic Beer: *He's poor and wants to get laid.*

Good Beer: *He likes good beer and wants to get laid.*

Wine: *He's hoping that the wine thing will give him a sophisticated image to help him get laid.*

Whiskey: *He doesn't give two shits about anything but getting laid.*

Tequila: *Piss off, all you wankers, I'm gonna go shag something.*

White Zin: *He's gay.*

Devotion
VODKA
Infused with Casein

Devoted Bull
Devotion Vodka,
Red Bull,
Spash of Cranberry.

Guiltless Cosmo
Devotion Vodka,
Triple Sec, Lime &
Cranberry Juice.

Protein Bar
Devotion Vodka,
Kahlua, Baileys
& Frangelico.

Golden Gate
Devotion Vodka,
7up, Orange Juice,
Melon Liqueur.

Love & Devotion
Devotion Vodka &
Raspberry Liqueur.

Devotion Potion
Devotion Vodka, Amaretto,
Peach Schnapps, OJ
& Cranberry Juice.

Get Devoted

twitter.com/devotionvodka   devotionvodka.com   facebook.com/devotionvodka

ABOUT THE AUTHOR

Johnny Metheny, aka Johnny Love, former owner of a series of bar and grills in California called Johnny Love's (hot spots of music, spirits, fine cuisine and good times,) is one of San Francisco's best know bartenders and a seasoned expert on the night life scene. Metheny got his nickname,

—Johnny Love", while a freshman at the University of California, Berkeley. He received his degree in Economics from Cal, was a member of three national championship rugby teams, and became a licensed stockbroker, but his true calling has been as bartender, club owner, and purveyor of fine spirits. Metheny was inducted into The Bartender's Hall of Fame by Bartender's Magazine. Despite his busy schedule, Metheny has pursued his interest in charitable causes. In 1991, he was named Leukemia Man Of The Year for being the top fund-raiser. Beginning in 1995, Metheny began working on a new super premium vodka, with the goal of popularizing American vodkas. He began infusing natural flavors into vodkas to sell at his restaurants and clubs. In 2004, Metheny sold his restaurants and clubs to launch Johnny Love Vodka, a line of flavored and ultra premium American vodkas, _www. johnnylovevodka.com._

In 2009, Metheny partnered in the launch of the first protein infused vodka, Devotion, that has the star of Jersey Shore, Mike —The Situation" Sorrentino as a partner / spokesman.

Metheny also finished writing a screenplay about 4 guys that bartend together in San Francisco. He completed the filming of the movie and it won awards in film festivals, www.itsallinanightswork. com. In addition, his late night TV show, *The Last Shot*, premiered in the San Francisco Bay Area on the WB Network, www.thelastshot.com.

He finished a new book, titled —Guide To Bar Etiquette", that is a humorous look at the things bar customers unknowingly do that annoys / angers...bartenders, waiters, bouncers and other bar staff.

For more information or to send any drink recipes (or things that bar customers shouldn't do), that are not in the book, please email Johnny at Johnnymetheny@yahoo.com